This book belongs to:

____

Aries Daily Horoscope 2025

Author's Note: Time set to Coordinated Universal Time Zone (UT±0)

Mystic Cat
Suite 41906, 3/2237 Gold Coast HWY
Mermaid Beach, Queensland, 4218
Australia
islandauthor@hotmail.com

The information accessible from this book is for informational purposes only. No statement within is a promise of benefits. There is no guarantee of any results.

Images are under license from Shutterstock, Dreamstime, Canva, or Deposit-photos.

Contents

The 12 Zodiac Star Signs

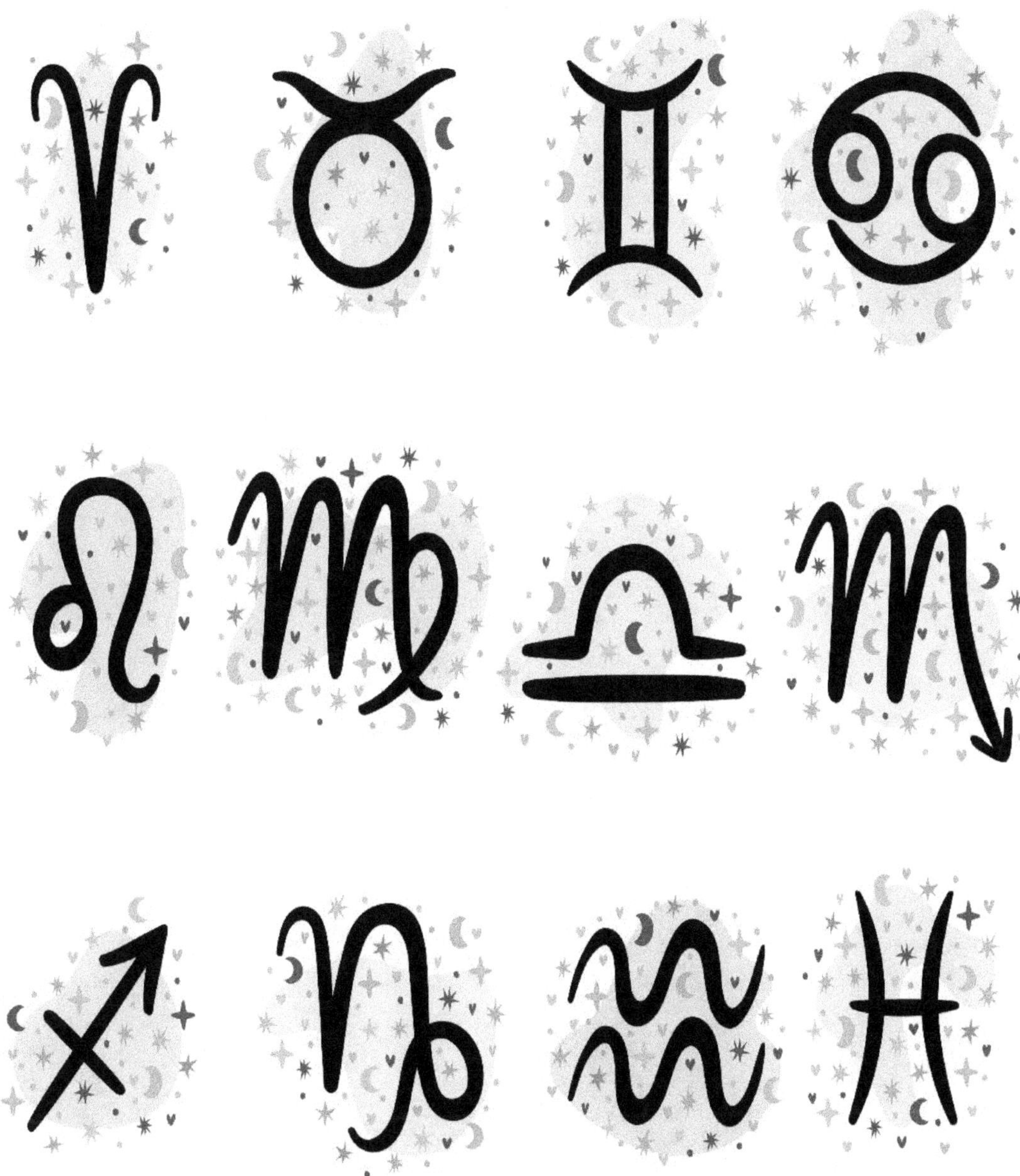

2025

January

S	M	T	W	T	F	S
			1	2	3	4
5	6	7	8	9	10	11
12	13	14	15	16	17	18
19	20	21	22	23	24	25
26	27	28	29	30	31	

February

S	M	T	W	T	F	S
						1
2	3	4	5	6	7	8
9	10	11	12	13	14	15
16	17	18	19	20	21	22
23	24	25	26	27	28	

March

S	M	T	W	T	F	S
						1
2	3	4	5	6	7	8
9	10	11	12	13	14	15
16	17	18	19	20	21	22
23	24	25	26	27	28	29
30	31					

April

S	M	T	W	T	F	S
		1	2	3	4	5
6	7	8	9	10	11	12
13	14	15	16	17	18	19
20	21	22	23	24	25	26
27	28	29	30			

May

S	M	T	W	T	F	S
				1	2	3
4	5	6	7	8	9	10
11	12	13	14	15	16	17
18	19	20	21	22	23	24
25	26	27	28	29	30	31

June

S	M	T	W	T	F	S
1	2	3	4	5	6	7
8	9	10	11	12	13	14
15	16	17	18	19	20	21
22	23	24	25	26	27	28
29	30					

July

S	M	T	W	T	F	S
		1	2	3	4	5
6	7	8	9	10	11	12
13	14	15	16	17	18	19
20	21	22	23	24	25	26
27	28	29	30	31		

August

S	M	T	W	T	F	S
					1	2
3	4	5	6	7	8	9
10	11	12	13	14	15	16
17	18	19	20	21	22	23
24	25	26	27	28	29	30
31						

September

S	M	T	W	T	F	S
	1	2	3	4	5	6
7	8	9	10	11	12	13
14	15	16	17	18	19	20
21	22	23	24	25	26	27
28	29	30				

October

S	M	T	W	T	F	S
			1	2	3	4
5	6	7	8	9	10	11
12	13	14	15	16	17	18
19	20	21	22	23	24	25
26	27	28	29	30	31	

November

S	M	T	W	T	F	S
						1
2	3	4	5	6	7	8
9	10	11	12	13	14	15
16	17	18	19	20	21	22
23	24	25	26	27	28	29
30						

December

S	M	T	W	T	F	S
	1	2	3	4	5	6
7	8	9	10	11	12	13
14	15	16	17	18	19	20
21	22	23	24	25	26	27
28	29	30	31			

2025

Daily Horoscope

As your astrologer, I wish to explain why one horoscope book may differ from another for each zodiac sign. The vast array of astrological activity constantly occurring in the sky requires me to focus on the essential aspect of the star sign I am writing for on any given day. Each zodiac sign is unique, and the various planetary factors affect them differently.

When crafting horoscopes, I pay special attention to the significant astrological aspects directly impacting a specific sign. By doing so, I can provide the most insightful and relevant guidance to individuals of that zodiac sign. While there might be multiple planetary alignments on a particular day, one aspect may hold more significance for a specific sign than others.

Considering the ruling planets and elements associated with each zodiac sign further refines my interpretations. This attention to detail ensures that the horoscope resonates with the distinct characteristics and tendencies of the star sign in question.

Ultimately, I aim to offer personalized insights and advice based on each zodiac sign's unique cosmic influences. By focusing on each star sign's most relevant astrological aspects, I can help readers better understand themselves and navigate the energies surrounding them. Embracing each zodiac sign's strengths, challenges, and opportunities allows me to create a horoscope book tailored to my readers' needs.

"We are born at a given moment, in a given place, and, like vintage years of wine, we have the qualities of the year and the season of which we are born. Astrology does not lay claim to anything more."

—Carl Jung

JANUARY

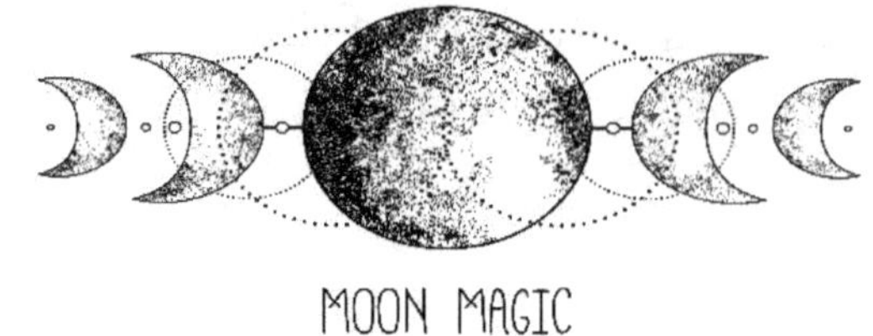

Sun	Mon	Tue	Wed	Thu	Fri	Sat
			1	2	3	4
5	6	7	8	9	10	11
12	13	14	15	16	17	18
19	20	21	22	23	24	25
26	27	28	29	30	31	

NEW MOON

Wolf Moon

30 Monday

With the Moon ingress Capricorn and the arrival of the New Moon, you may experience a shift towards a more disciplined and structured approach in your life. This alignment is a time for setting goals, planning, and taking practical steps toward achieving them. You may feel renewed determination and desire to build a solid foundation for your future. It's an excellent time to focus on your career or long-term ambitions and take steps toward success.

31 Tuesday

The future is seen through a lens of limitless potential. Focusing on developing your social life leads to enriching encounters where shared ideas kindle vibrant energy. As you gently weave changes into your life, the stable foundations you establish will provide the scaffolding for an era of thoughtful discussions, breathing life into your manifestations. Open and honest communication will promote the development of deeper emotional connections.

1 Wednesday

This New Year's Day, with the Moon entering Aquarius, you may feel a surge of innovative and forward-thinking energy. You feel drawn to group activities that promote a sense of unity. It's an excellent opportunity to connect with and expand your network. The influence of this lunar phase encourages you to think outside the box and explore unconventional ideas and approaches. Embrace your independence and let your creativity flow as you set intentions for the year ahead.

2 Thursday

As you shed the backdrop of the past, you'll embrace a lighter, more refreshing surge of energy. Incoming news bears fruit, presenting an opportunity to venture into uncharted territories that offer room for your life to flourish. As you dive into this fresh avenue of possibility, you'll encounter like-minded individuals who share your goals. This group dynamic fosters insightful discussions and supportive dialogues, facilitating a learning experience that expands life.

3 Friday

As Venus enters Pisces, you may experience heightened compassion and sensitivity in your relationships. This transit encourages you to connect deeply with others emotionally and seek harmony and understanding. It's a time to embrace empathy and express love in gentle and nurturing ways. Meanwhile, the opposition between Mars and Pluto can bring intensity and power struggles. It's essential to be mindful and find constructive ways to channel your energy.

4 Saturday

The Sun forms a sextile aspect with Saturn, bringing an opportunity to harness discipline, perseverance, and practicality to achieve your goals. This alignment brings a sense of stability and structure to your life, allowing you to make steady progress and build a solid foundation for success. Embracing this harmonious connection between the Sun and Saturn creates a sense of accomplishment and self-confidence.

5 Sunday

As the Moon enters Aries, you may experience a surge of energy and assertiveness in your emotional state. This fiery and passionate energy inspires you to take the initiative, be more self-directed, and enthusiastically pursue your desires. This transit encourages you to be courageous, bold, and spontaneous in expressing your emotions and taking action. It's a time to embrace your inner warrior and fearlessly go after what you want.

January

6 Monday

With Mars entering Cancer, you may notice a shift in your assertiveness and drive as your focus turns towards nurturing and protecting what is important to you. This energy encourages you to take action from an emotional standpoint, relying on your intuition and sensitivity to guide your decisions. Your motivation is rooted in creating a sense of emotional security and establishing a harmonious environment.

7 Tuesday

As the Moon enters Taurus, you may experience a shift in your emotional landscape towards stability and comfort. This influence encourages you to seek security and pleasure in simple joys. Your emotions are grounded and focused on practical matters like finances, possessions, and physical well-being. You draw activities that bring you a sense of security and inner peace, such as enjoying good food, surrounding yourself with beauty, or connecting with nature.

8 Wednesday

With Mercury entering Capricorn, you enter a period of focused and practical thinking. Your mind becomes more disciplined and organized, allowing you to approach tasks and challenges strategically. You're likely to prioritize efficiency and long-term goals, seeking to make practical decisions based on facts and logic. Communication becomes more structured and deliberate as you value clarity and precision in your interactions.

9 Thursday

Changes on the horizon usher in a creative and healing journey, unveiling unique opportunities that expand your life's tapestry. Embrace this creative phase that fuels expansion as you utilize your innate talents to fuel your growth. A vibrant social environment beckons, inviting you to mingle and network. The path you're embarking on is worth the effort, and the more you engage with life, the more it meets you with opportunities that truly deserve your time and energy.

January

10 Friday

With the Moon entering Gemini, you experience a shift in emotional energy and a heightened sense of curiosity and mental stimulation. Your emotions become more adaptable and changeable, reflecting the versatile nature of Gemini. You may seek intellectual stimulation and crave social interactions that engage your mind. This transit encourages you to be open-minded and flexible in your emotional responses, allowing various perspectives and ideas to flow.

11 Saturday

A shift in perspective heralds romance and deeper connections, opening the door to a chapter filled with companionship. This fresh outlook brings a revitalizing landscape that fosters renewal and well-being—investing time in strengthening personal bonds ushers in promising opportunities that lead to a broader horizon of possibilities. Connecting with kindred spirits who share your outlook on life will set the stage for a thrilling journey ahead.

12 Sunday

With the Moon entering Cancer and Mars forming a trine aspect with Neptune, you may experience a deepening of your emotional sensitivity and a harmonious alignment between your actions and your dreams. This transit invites you to tap into your intuition and connect with your emotions. You may find that your instincts guide you towards nurturing and caring for yourself and others, as the Cancer energy encourages a focus on home, family, and emotional well-being.

13 Monday

With the Sun forming a trine with Uranus and a Full Moon illuminating the sky, you are entering a period of excitement, liberation, and heightened awareness. The Sun trine Uranus aspect infuses your life with a sense of individuality, innovation, and the desire for freedom. You may break free from routines and embrace new and unconventional ways of expressing yourself. This alignment encourages you to embrace your unique qualities and explore new possibilities.

14 Tuesday

With the Moon entering Leo and Venus forming a square aspect with Jupiter, you are entering a period of heightened passion, creativity, and expansive emotions. The Moon's ingress into Leo ignites a spark within you, encouraging self-expression, confidence, and a desire for recognition. You long to be seen and appreciated for your unique qualities. This lunar energy fuels your creativity and encourages you to engage in activities that bring you joy and fulfillment.

15 Wednesday

Exploring new avenues generates leads that offer rising prospects, enabling you to chart a course toward improved circumstances. This highly productive cycle unlocks the floodgates to a lighter, more hopeful energy, marking a significant turning point as you fortify the foundations of your life. An imminent upgrade sets you on a winning trajectory, infusing your life with positive and inspirational energy. This awakening to possibilities guides you toward unprecedented growth.

16 Thursday

With the Sun opposing Mars and the Moon entering Virgo, you may experience a dynamic interplay between assertiveness and practicality. The Sun's opposition to Mars brings an energy that can fuel motivation and a desire to take action. However, this aspect also carries the potential for impulsive behavior and a tendency to rush without considering the consequences. As the Moon moves into Virgo, it brings a grounding influence that encourages a focus on organization.

17 Friday

With the Sun sextile Neptune, this harmonious aspect allows for a gentle flow of energy between your conscious self and the ethereal realm of Neptune. You will likely feel more attuned to your intuition and sensitive to the subtle energies around you. This aspect encourages you to tap into your creative abilities and explore artistic or spiritual pursuits. It's a time when your imagination can soar, and you may find inspiration in the beauty and mysticism of the world.

18 Saturday

Breaking news arrives at your doorstep, ushering in fresh opportunities. These developments beckon you to connect with a broader social sphere, providing a sturdy foundation to expand your world. Expanding your social circle injects vivacity and excitement into your life, reaching crescendo levels. Cultivating these connections fosters happiness and harmony, providing the stable footing from which you can confidently tread forward.

19 Sunday

With Venus conjunct Saturn, you may experience a period of increased seriousness and focus in your relationships and personal values. This alignment encourages you to take a more disciplined and responsible approach to matters of the heart. You seek stability and long-term commitment, prioritizing loyalty and reliability in your interactions. As the Moon ingresses Libra, your emotional landscape becomes more balanced, and you strive for harmony and fairness.

20 Monday

Your social landscape is poised for an upward swing, bringing companionship and camaraderie your way. As puzzle pieces fall into place, a journey of happiness unfolds, rejuvenating your energy and spirit. You'll find yourself aligning with individuals who wholeheartedly support your growth and evolution, creating an enchanting backdrop for an adventurous and exhilarating expansion. A newfound sense of joy takes flight within you, acting as a gentle breeze beneath your wings.

21 Tuesday

As the Moon ingresses Scorpio, it intensifies your emotions and adds depth and introspection to your inner world. You may find yourself drawn to investigate the mysteries of life and engage in soul-searching activities. Your inner strength can see you face fears and embrace the process of personal metamorphosis. It is a time for self-discovery and embracing transformative power. Allow yourself to navigate the depths of your emotions and trust in growth and regeneration.

22 Wednesday

Embarking on a journey of exploration triggers a new route, illuminating a path to progress. This transformation marks a significant turning point, allowing you to nurture your skills and extend your reach into uncharted territory. Your optimistic spirit is a golden key, unlocking a treasure trove of possibilities. Stirring the potent essence of manifestation unleashes a whirlwind of opportunities, marking a dynamic period rich with pioneering options.

23 Thursday

With Mars sextile Uranus, you may feel a surge of dynamic energy and a desire for change and excitement. This aspect ignites a spark of innovation and boldness within you, urging you to take courageous action and pursue your individuality. It's a time to embrace your unique ideas and approach tasks with a sense of adventure and spontaneity. As Mercury opposes Mars, there may be a tendency for conflicts of opinion. It's important to stay mindful of your communication.

24 Friday

With the Moon ingress Sagittarius, you may experience a sense of adventure and a desire for exploration. This aspect brings light and optimistic energy into your life, inspiring you to broaden your horizons and seek new experiences. You may feel a strong pull towards expanding your knowledge through travel, higher education, or philosophical pursuits. It's a time to embrace your freedom and independence and pursue opportunities that resonate with your inner truth.

25 Saturday

With Venus trine Mars, you experience a harmonious blending of feminine and masculine energies within you. This aspect brings a sense of balance and harmony to your relationships and personal desires. You may feel more confident and assertive in expressing your romantic and creative urges. Your passions ignite, and you have a natural charm that attracts others to you. This transit is an excellent time to pursue your passions, whether in love, art, or any creative endeavor.

26 Sunday

With the Moon ingress Capricorn, you enter a focused determination and practicality period. Your emotions align with your ambitions, and you feel the drive to achieve your goals with discipline and perseverance. This lunar influence encourages you to take a structured and organized approach to your endeavors, allowing you to make steady progress toward your objectives. It's a busy period that invites you to embrace growth, exploration, and the manifestation of dreams.

27 Monday

Anticipate a series of enhancements that herald a time of setting long-term aspirations into motion. As you shape and nurture dreams, your surroundings become a bustling, productive hub, propelling you toward advancement. Your diligent efforts to enhance your circumstances yield bountiful rewards. Your meticulous attention to detail sparks a journey ripe with possibilities, offering the space needed to cultivate goals that channel your energy toward a brighter future.

28 Tuesday

With Mercury ingress Aquarius, your thinking and communication take on a more progressive and innovative tone. You become open to new ideas and perspectives, valuing intellectual freedom and individuality. Your mind becomes attuned to collective thinking and humanitarian ideals, making you more interested in social causes and group dynamics. You may draw unconventional concepts and discussions that challenge traditional norms.

29 Wednesday

With Mercury conjunct with Pluto, you delve into the realms of power, transformation, and the mysteries of the mind. This aspect enhances your ability to uncover hidden truths and go beneath the surface, allowing you to gain insight and understanding. Your words carry weight and influence; you may draw research, investigation, and uncover secrets. This conjunction encourages you to dig deep, question assumptions, and explore the depths of your psyche.

30 Thursday

With Uranus turning direct, a surge of revolutionary energy awakens within you. This planetary shift signals breaking free from limitations and embracing your unique individuality. You may feel a strong urge to shake up the status quo and explore new horizons. It's a period of personal liberation and embracing your authentic self. Coupled with the Moon's ingress into Pisces, your emotions become fluid and deeply connected to the cosmic flow.

FEBRUARY

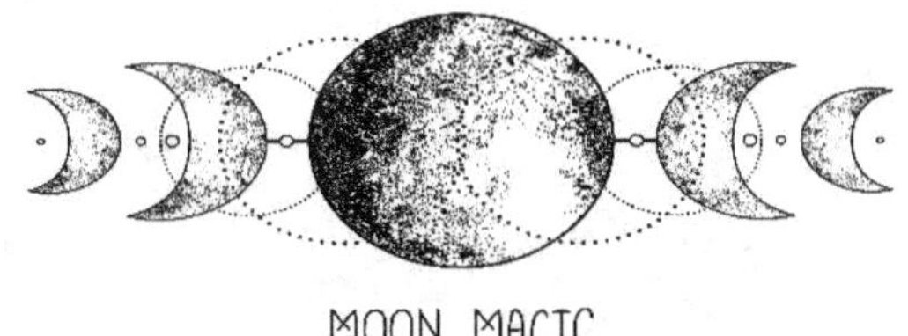

Sun	Mon	Tue	Wed	Thu	Fri	Sat
						1
2	3	4	5	6	7	8
9	10	11	12	13	14	15
16	17	18	19	20	21	22
23	24	25	26	27	28	

New Moon

Snow Moon

31 Friday

Gorgeous transformations gracefully flow, introducing fresh options and igniting a sense of movement and exploration. These changes promise an exhilarating journey, liberating you from existing constraints and guiding you towards a horizon of rising possibilities. You're embarking on a delightful adventure, delving into new interests that align with kindred spirits who share your wavelength, and expanding your circle of friends into a rich tapestry of possibilities.

1 Saturday

With Venus conjunct Neptune, you enter a dreamy and enchanting realm of heightened sensitivity and imagination. This celestial alignment invites you to explore love, beauty, and artistic expression. You may be captivated by romantic ideals, seeking deeper connections, and yearning for soulful experiences. It's a time to let your heart lead and embrace the magic of love and compassion. Trust your intuition and let your creative spirit soar.

2 Sunday

With the Moon shifting into Aries, you feel a surge of fiery energy and assertiveness within you. This ingress brings a sense of boldness and enthusiasm to your emotions and actions. You may be eager to initiate new projects, take on challenges, and assert individuality. The Aries Moon encourages you to embrace your independence and pursue your passions with courage and determination. It's a time to trust your instincts and embrace spontaneity.

FEBRUARY

3 Monday

With Mercury forming a harmonious trine aspect to Jupiter, you receive a powerful boost of intellectual prowess and expansive thinking. This alignment brings a period of enhanced communication, optimism, and broad-mindedness. Your mind is open to new possibilities, and your ideas flow effortlessly. You can express yourself clearly and enthusiastically, captivating others with wisdom and insight. Embrace this cosmic alignment as it encourages abundant possibilities.

4 Tuesday

With the Moon entering Taurus, Venus moving into Aries, and Jupiter turning direct, you are entering a period of powerful energetic shifts and forward momentum. The stable and grounded influence of the Moon in Taurus brings a sense of comfort, security, and a deep connection to your physical senses. You can indulge in self-care and enjoy the pleasures of life. Simultaneously, Venus in Aries ignites your passion and desire in relationships and creative endeavors.

5 Wednesday

Prepare to lift the lid on an expansive journey that amplifies prospects in your life. This blossoming period invites you to chase your dreams and cultivate remarkable goals. It guides you towards an approach that fosters enrichment and progression. Engaging in discussions opens doors to positive prospects, paving the way for developing longer-term goals and ushering in a dynamic and active phase that redefines what's possible in your life.

6 Thursday

As the Moon moves into Gemini, you enter a period of intellectual curiosity and heightened communication. This energy stimulates your mind and encourages you to explore new ideas, engage in stimulating conversations, and seek out knowledge. Your thoughts become agile and adaptable, allowing you to quickly adapt to changing circumstances and connect with others on a mental level. This transit is a good time for networking, learning, and gathering information.

FEBRUARY

7 Friday

With Venus forming a harmonious sextile aspect to Pluto, you delve into the depths of your relationships and uncover hidden passions. This alignment ignites a transformative energy within your connections, deepening intimacy and emotional growth. You can explore the layers of your desires and connect profoundly with your loved ones. This aspect brings forth a magnetic attraction and intensifies the power of love and passion in your life.

8 Saturday

With the Moon moving into Cancer, your emotional landscape becomes more sensitive and nurturing. You may find comfort and security in the familiar and the warmth of your loved ones. This lunar ingress invites you to connect with your emotions and honor your intuitive guidance. It's a time to prioritize self-care and create a haven within your home and personal space. Trust your instincts and listen to your feelings as they guide you to understand your needs and desires.

9 Sunday

With the Sun and Mercury aligning, there is a harmonious fusion between your core identity and your thought processes. This alignment empowers you to express yourself with clarity, confidence, and authenticity. It's a time to trust your intellect and intuition as you make important decisions and pursue your goals. Meanwhile, the Mars trine Saturn aspect balances assertiveness and discipline. This aspect helps you channel your passion and drive into productive endeavors.

February

10 Monday

As the Moon moves into Leo, you experience a surge of confidence and self-expression. This astrological transit ignites your inner fire and encourages you to shine brightly. You radiate charisma and magnetism, drawing others towards your vibrant energy. Your emotions are more passionate and playful, fueling your creativity and desire for enjoyment. It's a time to embrace individuality and express yourself authentically without fear of judgment or reprisal.

11 Tuesday

When the Sun forms a square aspect with Uranus, you may experience unexpected changes and disruptions. This aspect brings a sense of restlessness and a desire for freedom and individuality. You may find yourself seeking new experiences, pushing boundaries, and challenging the status quo. It's a time to embrace your unique identity and break free from limitations. Opportunities for personal growth and self-discovery arise from embracing the unexpected.

12 Wednesday

The Sun and Moon are in opposition during a Full Moon, creating a powerful, energetic culmination. This phase invites you to bring awareness to the fruition of your intentions and the illumination of hidden parts. It is a time of heightened emotions and clarity, where feelings magnify, and insights can surface. The Full Moon acts as a mirror, reflecting on your progress and highlighting areas where growth and release are needed.

13 Thursday

As the Moon moves into Virgo, practical and analytical energy permeates the atmosphere. This shift focuses on organization, efficiency, and attention to detail. You may find yourself drawn to tidying up your physical and mental spaces, seeking clarity and structure in your daily routines. The Virgo influence encourages you to be diligent, discerning, and dedicated to your tasks. It's an excellent time to assess goals, make plans, and take steps toward achieving them.

FEBRUARY

14 Friday

As Mercury moves into Pisces, there is a shift toward sensitivity, intuition, and emotional connection in your communication style. This transit invites you to tap into your compassionate and empathetic nature, allowing you to express your thoughts and feelings with greater depth and understanding. You may find yourself more inclined to listen attentively to others. Embrace the power of words and express your love and affection in heartfelt and imaginative ways.

15 Saturday

As the Moon moves into Libra, you can embrace a harmonious and balanced approach to life. This transit brings a heightened awareness of your relationships and the importance of finding equilibrium in your interactions. You may feel a greater desire to seek fairness and compromise, valuing diplomacy and cooperation in your connections. This planetary transit is an ideal time to engage in activities that promote peace and harmony.

16 Sunday

New opportunities gracefully usher companionship and harmony into your world, marking the dawn of an engaging chapter in your personal life that dismantles barriers and unveils an exciting path forward. It's the commencement of an enriching journey, presenting rising prospects in your romantic life. Thoughtful discussions lay the groundwork for grounded foundations, igniting progress and joy.

17 Monday

An upsurge of opportunities within your social sphere ushers in a stylish and expansive chapter, initiating a daring journey brimming with excitement and liberation. Unexpected communications arrive, brilliantly steering you towards a passionate and adventurous expedition. Inspiration gracefully envelops your social landscape, bestowing you newfound confidence and a willingness to broaden your circle of friends.

18 Tuesday

Intense emotions and deep introspection may come to the forefront of your experience as the Moon moves into Scorpio. You may find yourself delving into the depths of your psyche, seeking a greater understanding of your desires and motivations. This cosmic alignment is a time of heightened sensitivity and intuition, allowing you to perceive the hidden truths beneath the surface. You may explore the mysteries of life and connect with your innermost passions.

19 Wednesday

This dynamic chapter allows your talents to shine brightly, propelling your abilities to new heights. Productivity becomes your ally, yielding gratifying results as you navigate uncharted pathways that bring visionary ideas, unveiling the boundless potential awaiting you. Now is the perfect time to focus on unearthing novel avenues that promise growth. With each step, you'll discover a delightful cadence that nurtures balance and stability, enticing movement and discovery.

20 Thursday

As the Moon moves into Sagittarius and Mercury forms a square aspect with Jupiter, you find yourself in a period of expansive energy and intellectual stimulation. Sagittarius' influence brings a sense of adventure and a desire for exploration. You are encouraged to broaden your horizons, seek new experiences, and expand your knowledge and understanding of the world. However, the square between Mercury and Jupiter challenges communication and decision-making.

21 Friday

Picture this: a celestial dance unfolds, casting a sparkling tapestry of potential across your path. The energies align to propel you forward into an enchanting chapter of exploration. With each step, you'll feel the exhilaration of newfound horizons beckoning you to chase your dreams. Your passions will be your guiding star, leading you to a future filled with the promise of endless joy. As the cosmic curtains rise, prepare to step onto a stage of profound and boundless potential.

22 Saturday

As the Moon enters Capricorn, you can embrace a more disciplined and structured approach to life. Capricorn brings a sense of practicality, responsibility, and ambition to the forefront of your consciousness. It is a time for setting goals, making plans, and taking concrete steps toward achieving them. You may focus more on your professional endeavors and long-term aspirations, seeking stability and success in your chosen path.

23 Sunday

The celestial clock is chiming, signaling a time of transformation and growth. The universe is like a guiding hand, leading you toward the experiences and encounters that will shape your destiny. You are the protagonist in your cosmic tale, and the chapters ahead are filled with excitement and wonder. Embrace the cosmic narrative, written in the language of possibility. As the cosmic currents flow, they carry you toward a future filled with promise and potential.

FEBRUARY

24 Monday

As Mars turns direct, a surge of dynamic energy propels you forward, igniting your drive and motivation. The period of retrograde reflection ends, allowing you to take decisive action and make tangible progress. This planetary shift encourages you to assert yourself, embrace courage, and overcome any obstacles that have held you back. With Mars Direct, you can tap into your inner warrior and channel your passion and determination into meaningful endeavors.

25 Tuesday

As the Moon ingresses into Aquarius, you may find yourself drawn to a more independent and intellectually stimulating approach to life. Your emotions align with a need for freedom, innovation, and community. This cosmic shift encourages you to embrace your unique perspective and seek unconventional ideas and solutions. Meanwhile, the conjunction of Mercury and Saturn brings a focused and disciplined mindset to your thoughts and communication.

26 Wednesday

A radiant shift is on the horizon, promising a wave of positive transformations. The universe is conspiring to usher in fresh beginnings and exciting possibilities. As you embrace this cosmic tide, you'll ride the crest of creativity, embarking on a journey where your talents flourish and your ambitions thrive. Keep your heart open; this is a time of bountiful opportunities and the potential for profound personal growth.

27 Thursday

As the Moon transitions into Pisces, you may feel a heightened sensitivity and emotional depth within yourself. This lunar energy invites you to tap into your intuition, imagination, and compassion. It's a time to embrace your inner world and explore creativity, spirituality, and empathy. Meanwhile, the sextile between Mercury and Uranus sparks a dynamic flow of ideas and intellectual stimulation. Your mind is open to innovation, allowing you to make unique connections.

March

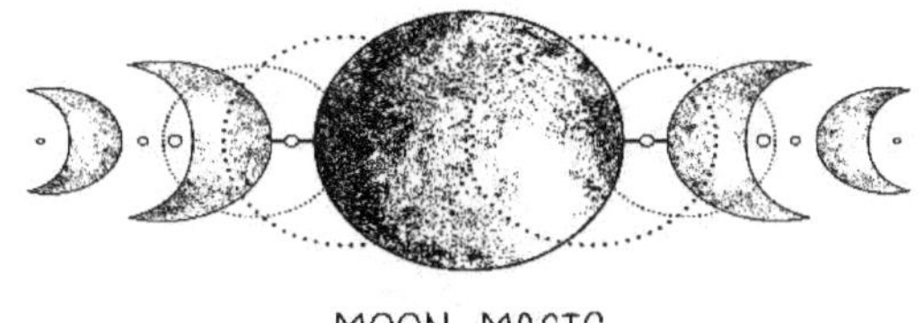

Sun	Mon	Tue	Wed	Thu	Fri	Sat
						1
2	3	4	5	6	7	8
9	10	11	12	13	14	15
16	17	18	19	20	21	22
23	24	25	26	27	28	29
30	31					

New Moon

WORM MOON

FEBRUARY/MARCH

28 Friday

As the New Moon arrives, it signals a fresh start and a blank canvas for you to manifest your intentions and set new goals. This lunar phase invites you to embrace the energy of beginnings and plant the seeds of your dreams. It's a potent time to reflect on what you truly desire and to visualize the life you want to create. With the darkness of the Moon, there is an invitation to go inward, to listen to your inner voice, and to trust your instincts.

1 Saturday

As the Moon enters Aries, you feel renewed energy, motivation, and assertiveness. This fiery lunar energy ignites your passion and drive, inspiring you to take action and enthusiastically pursue your goals. It's a time to embrace individuality and confidently express your authentic self. The Aries Moon empowers you to be bold, courageous, and adventurous. Use this time to assert your independence, pursue your passions, and ignite the flame of inspiration.

2 Sunday

As Venus moves retrograde, you may reflect on matters of the heart and reevaluate your relationships and values. This introspective period invites you to revisit past experiences and explore the deeper layers of your emotions. Mercury conjunct Neptune lets you tap into your creative potential and gain insights from dreams and inspiration. However, the Sun square Jupiter can bring the need to balance expanding your horizons and maintaining a realistic perspective.

MARCH

3 Monday

As Mercury ingresses Aries, your thoughts and communication style become more direct and assertive. You may feel a surge of energy and enthusiasm, prompting you to speak your mind and take action. Trust your instincts and embrace a spontaneous approach in your interactions. With the Moon ingress Taurus, you may seek comfort, stability, and sensual pleasures. It's an excellent time to focus on well-being and indulge in the simple pleasures that bring you joy.

4 Tuesday

The universe invites you to harness your inner potential and seize growth opportunities. Your days are filled with purpose and progress as you make strides in your professional and academic journey. Trust in the cosmic guidance, and your midweek will be a beacon of accomplishment. The celestial energies align to boost your intellect and work ethic. Your life becomes a stage for intellectual prowess and professional excellence.

5 Wednesday

With the Moon's ingress into Gemini, your mind becomes curious and adaptable, seeking intellectual stimulation and variety. You'll likely experience a desire to engage in lively conversations and exchange ideas. This energy supports you in being more flexible and open-minded, allowing you to navigate different perspectives and explore new concepts. Mercury's sextile to Pluto adds depth to your communication. You possess the ability to delve into profound subjects.

6 Thursday

The universe bestows a gift of productivity and clarity, allowing you to tackle tasks with precision and purpose. Each day becomes a stepping stone towards your goals, and life is a testament to your dedication and determination. As you navigate the landscape, cosmic energies converge to enhance your world. It's as if the universe is opening a treasure trove of knowledge and opportunity before you. Life becomes a journey of discovery, offering a chance to expand your horizons.

7 Friday

With the Moon moving into Cancer, you may find yourself in a more emotionally sensitive and nurturing state. Your focus shifts towards your inner world and the needs of your heart. You may feel a longing for comfort, security, and familiar surroundings. This aspect is a time to honor your emotions and create a safe space for yourself to explore and express your feelings. You may find solace in connecting with loved ones and creating a sense of home and belonging.

8 Saturday

With the Sun forming a harmonious trine aspect to Mars, you may experience a surge of energy, motivation, and assertiveness. This alignment ignites a sense of confidence and drive, empowering you to take action and pursue your goals enthusiastically. You feel a strong sense of vitality and purpose, propelling you forward in your endeavors. This favorable alignment enhances your ability to assert yourself and progress in various areas of your life.

9 Sunday

Today's lunar transit encourages you to embrace uniqueness and express yourself authentically. You may seek attention as you yearn to be seen and appreciated. It's a time to indulge in activities that bring out your inner child and allow your vibrant personality to radiate. Let your passions and creativity take center stage and bask in the limelight of your unique essence. Embrace the lunar energy in Leo to express yourself and embrace your inner fire confidently.

March

10 Monday

Imagine the cosmos as your life coach, guiding you toward success in work and studies. The celestial energies align to boost your productivity and determination. Your days are filled with purpose and achievement as you excel in your professional and academic pursuits. Embrace the cosmic mentorship, and watch as your week becomes a testament to your accomplishments. Trust in the heavenly partnership, and success will be your companion.

11 Tuesday

When Mercury and Venus come together, it brings a harmonious blend of communication and love into your life. Your words become infused with warmth, charm, and grace, making it easier for you to express your affections and connect with others on a deeper level. This alignment enhances your ability to express your feelings, thoughts, and desires with clarity and diplomacy, allowing for smoother and more enjoyable interactions.

12 Wednesday

As the Moon moves into Virgo and aligns with the Sun in conjunction with Saturn, you may feel a sense of grounding and practicality sweeping over you. This alignment encourages you to consider your responsibilities, commitments, and long-term goals. It's a time to focus on organization, efficiency, and attending to the details of your life. You can bring structure and discipline to your daily routines, helping you progress and achieve your objectives.

13 Thursday

As you navigate life's journey, the cosmic energies align to enhance your overall experience. The universe acts as your silent partner, steering you towards moments of growth and personal discovery. Your life becomes a symphony of achievements, with each note representing your resilience and determination. Trust in cosmic guidance and your overall life will flourish. The celestial energies align to boost your ambition and drive.

March

14 Friday

During the Full Moon phase, the Sun forms a harmonious sextile with Uranus while the Moon enters Libra, creating a dynamic and transformative energy in your life. This alignment encourages you to embrace change, innovation, and the pursuit of personal freedom. You can break from old patterns and explore new possibilities that align with your authentic self. The Full Moon illuminates areas that require balance and harmony, particularly in relationships and partnerships.

15 Saturday

As Mercury turns retrograde, you are encouraged to slow down, review, and reflect. This celestial event signals a period of introspection and introspection in your communication, thinking, and decision-making processes. It's a time to pay attention to details, be mindful of miscommunications, and avoid rushing into new ventures. Take this opportunity to revisit past projects, reconnect with old acquaintances, and reassess your plans and goals.

16 Sunday

Picture the universe as your social coordinator, creating opportunities for connection and celebration. The celestial energies align to boost your sociability and charm. The divine energies align to encourage warmth and hospitality. Your weekend becomes a tapestry of joyful gatherings and heartwarming moments as you cherish the bonds with friends and loved ones. Embrace the cosmic festivities, and watch as your social life flourishes.

17 Monday

You may feel the heightened intensity and emotional depth as the Moon moves into Scorpio. It is a time when you can delve into the hidden realms of your psyche and explore your innermost desires and passions. The energy of Scorpio encourages you to embrace transformation and seek truth and authenticity in your life. You may find yourself drawn to activities that involve introspection, self-reflection, and personal growth.

18 Tuesday

As you navigate, cosmic energies converge to enhance your overall experience. It's as if the universe is opening doors to new opportunities and profound realizations. Life becomes a journey of self-discovery and personal growth, with each day offering a chance to expand your horizons and find deeper meaning. Life is a cosmic adventure, with the celestial forces aligning to empower your sense of purpose. It's as though the universe has laid out a map of possibilities before you.

19 Wednesday

As the Moon enters Sagittarius, you may feel a sense of expansion and optimism within your emotional realm. Your spirits lift, and you seek new experiences and broaden your horizons. This lunar phase encourages you to embrace adventure and explore the unknown. With the Sun conjunct Neptune, a dreamy and imaginative energy permeates your being. It's a time to trust your intuition and listen to the subtle whispers of your soul.

20 Thursday

As the Sun enters Aries, marking the Vernal Equinox, a surge of energy and vitality courses through you. This celestial event signifies the beginning of a new astrological year, heralding a fresh start and a sense of rebirth. You may feel a strong urge to take action and pursue your goals with renewed enthusiasm. The Aries energy ignites your inner fire, empowering you to embrace individuality. It's a time to step with confidence and courage, embracing the spirit of initiative.

MARCH

21 Friday

You may experience a magnetic attraction or a strong emotional bond with someone, leading to profound personal growth and transformation. It's a time to delve into the shadows of your desires and uncover the hidden treasures within. Embrace the harmonious alignment between Venus and Pluto, and allow it to guide you towards profound emotional connections and experiences of deep love and empowerment.

22 Saturday

When the Moon ingresses Capricorn, you may feel a heightened sense of responsibility and a focus on achieving your goals. This energy brings a practical and disciplined approach to your emotions, urging you to prioritize stability and long-term success. You may find yourself drawn to tasks that require perseverance and a methodical mindset. This lunar influence encourages you to set clear intentions, make practical decisions, and take steps toward your ambitions.

23 Sunday

When the Sun is conjunct with Venus, and the Sun is also sextile with Pluto, you will likely experience a powerful blend of love, passion, and transformative energy. This cosmic alignment brings forth an opportunity to deepen your connections, enhance your relationships, and tap into your inner desires. You may feel a surge of creativity, confidence, and a magnetic charm that attracts positive experiences and meaningful connections.

March

24 Monday

When the Moon ingresses Aquarius and the Sun conjuncts Mercury, you may experience intellectual curiosity and a desire to explore new ideas and perspectives. Aquarius is an air sign associated with innovation, uniqueness, and progressive thinking. This energy encourages you to embrace your individuality as you may feel a strong need for freedom and independence, valuing your thoughts and opinions while being open to collaboration and collective thinking.

25 Tuesday

When Mercury sextiles Pluto, you have the potential to tap into profound depths of insight and understanding. This aspect allows you to delve into the mysteries of the mind, uncover hidden truths, and engage in transformative conversations. Your thoughts and communication carry intensity, allowing you to perceive beneath the surface and grasp the underlying dynamics. This aspect encourages you to research and investigate complex subjects with an analytical eye.

26 Wednesday

When the Moon ingresses Pisces, your intuition becomes heightened, and you're more attuned to the subtle energies around you. This aspect is a time to embrace your compassionate nature and connect deeply with others emotionally. You may desire to help those in need and offer support and understanding. It's a time for introspection and self-reflection as you explore the depths of your emotions and inner world.

27 Thursday

As the Black Moon enters Scorpio and Venus moves into Pisces, you may discover your desires and seek a deeper connection with your inner world. The energy becomes intense and mysterious, inviting you to explore the hidden realms of your psyche and confront any unresolved emotional patterns. With Venus conjunct Neptune, there is a sense of enchantment and allure, drawing you toward romantic fantasies and the realm of the imagination.

28 Friday

As the Moon enters Aries, fiery and passionate energy ignites within you. You reveal a renewed sense of enthusiasm and a drive to take action. It is a time of initiation and new beginnings, where you feel empowered to assert yourself and go after what you want. Your emotions fuel with courage and determination, and you are ready to face any challenges. Trust your instincts and embrace your inner warrior as you embark on this journey of self-discovery and personal growth.

29 Saturday

The New Moon presents you with a fresh start, a blank canvas upon which you can manifest your intentions and set new goals. This lunar phase marks a time of renewal and initiation, inviting you to plant the seeds of your desires and aspirations. It's an opportunity to reflect on your path and align your actions with your deepest aspirations. As the old fades away, you can shape your future and create the life you envision.

30 Sunday

As Mercury enters Pisces and joins forces with Neptune, your mind becomes attuned to the mystical and intuitive realms. It's a time when you hear the whispers of inspiration and the depths of your imagination. You may find yourself more in tune with your dreams, intuition, and the subtle energies surrounding you. This alignment invites you to explore creativity, spirituality, and inner reflection. As Neptune also transitions into Aries, a passion and self-discovery ignite within you.

APRIL

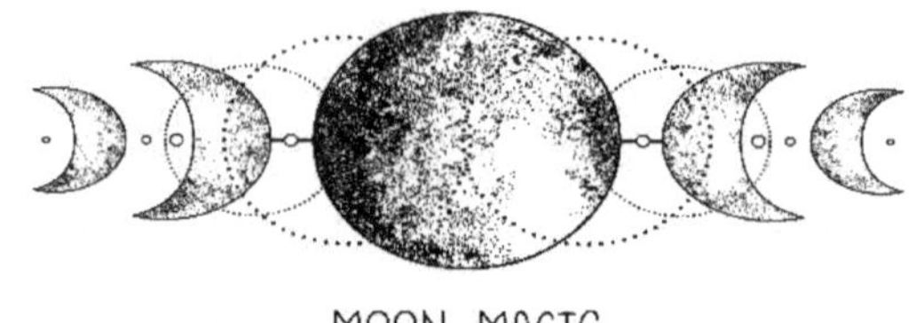

Sun	Mon	Tue	Wed	Thu	Fri	Sat
		1	2	3	4	5
6	7	8	9	10	11	12
13	14	15	16	17	18	19
20	21	22	23	24	25	26
27	28	29	30			

NEW MOON

PINK MOON

31 Monday

You currently navigate a transition phase, where emotions may surge, creating pockets of introspection. Yet, within this transformative period lies a healing influence reverberating throughout your life, offering the opportunity to make peace with your past. Embracing the wisdom that every experience contributes to the intricate mosaic of your life's journey enables you to gracefully shed outdated layers and create space for the brilliant tapestry of fresh possibilities.

1 Tuesday

As the Moon moves into Gemini, you feel light, and curiosity awakens. Your mind becomes agile and adaptable, ready to explore new ideas and engage in stimulating conversations. This lunar transit ignites your desire for intellectual growth and social interaction, encouraging you to connect with others intellectually. Let the Moon in Gemini inspire you to embrace the power of communication and curiosity, opening new doors of understanding.

2 Wednesday

The universe offers you a chance to reinvent yourself and explore uncharted territory. Your dreams and aspirations are within reach, and the cosmic energies are here to support you every step of the way. Embrace this heavenly gift, and watch your life become a beautiful tapestry of possibilities. You're poised to embark on self-discovery and transformation with the stars as your backdrop. It is your time to emerge from the cocoon of your comfort zone and spread your wings.

3 Thursday

As the Moon moves into Cancer, you may find yourself tapping into your emotional depths and seeking comfort and security in familiar surroundings. Your sensitivity and intuition heighten, allowing you to connect more deeply with your emotions. This lunar transit invites you to nurture yourself and those you care about, creating a nurturing and cozy atmosphere that feels like home. It's a time to honor feelings and seek solace in the familiar comforts of your personal space.

APRIL

4 Friday

With Saturn sextile Uranus and Mars sextile Uranus, you find yourself in a dynamic and harmonious energy that encourages stability and innovation. This aspect inspires you to balance tradition and progress, allowing you to embrace change while respecting the foundations you've built. You can combine your disciplined approach with a willingness to explore new possibilities and take calculated risks.

5 Saturday

With Mars forming a trine aspect to Saturn, you reveal a powerful combination of discipline and motivation. This harmonious alignment empowers you to take focused and deliberate action toward your goals. You possess the stamina and determination to overcome obstacles and make steady progress in your endeavors. The Mars trine Saturn aspect gives you the drive and perseverance to tackle challenging tasks and responsibilities.

6 Sunday

With the Moon entering Leo, you reveal vibrant and expressive energy. This lunar transit encourages you to shine brightly and embrace individuality. The Sun forming a harmonious sextile aspect with Jupiter amplifies your optimism. You are inspired to expand your horizons, explore new opportunities, and cultivate a positive mindset that fuels your growth. The Venus-Mars trine adds a touch of passion, harmony, and creative energy to your relationships and desires.

7 Monday

With Venus forming a conjunction with Saturn, you may experience a blend of practicality, stability, and commitment in your relationships and creative endeavors. This alignment brings a sense of seriousness and responsibility to your interactions and artistic pursuits. You may value loyalty, long-term commitments, and building solid foundations. This conjunction encourages you to approach matters of the heart with maturity and a willingness to create lasting connections.

8 Tuesday

With Venus forming a sextile aspect with Uranus, you may experience a delightful blend of excitement and harmony in your relationships and personal expression. This alignment brings an element of surprise, innovation, and uniqueness to your interactions, allowing you to explore new possibilities and embrace unconventional forms of love and beauty. You may find yourself drawn to people and experiences outside your usual comfort zone, igniting a sense of adventure.

9 Wednesday

As the celestial bodies weave their intricate dance through the cosmos, a profound transformation emerges on the horizon. Like the changing of seasons, you find yourself shedding the old and embracing the emergence of a newer, more authentic version of yourself. This cosmic shift brings forth opportunities akin to celestial gifts, opening the door to personal growth and positive change that ripples through the tapestry of your life.

10 Thursday

As communication arrives, Things are in motion, propelling you to develop a more prosperous social life. Life aligns favorably as mingling invitations bring harmony to your world, ushering in a time of thoughtful discussions and balanced foundations. Focusing on the most promising areas revamps your situation, leading you toward an abundant landscape of possibilities. Nurturing communication fosters growth as exciting invitations generate excitement.

APRIL

11 Friday

With the Moon ingress Libra, you may seek harmony, balance, and a sense of fairness in your emotional experiences. Your focus shifts towards creating harmonious relationships, cultivating diplomacy, and finding common ground with others. This lunar influence encourages you to consider different perspectives and weigh the pros and cons before deciding or taking action. You may feel more inclined to seek compromise and find the middle ground.

12 Saturday

By making your life the focal point, you set the stage for new growth pathways, each infused with the essence of inspiration. This conscious choice ushers in a social dimension, propelling you into an enriching environment with vibrant conversations and meaningful connections. In the blink of an eye, you'll naturally attract opportunities that harmonize with your vision for future expansion. Sharing moments with friends casts a warm glow on your path, expanding life.

13 Sunday

You may experience powerful emotions and intensity as the Full Moon illuminates the night sky. This lunar phase brings a culmination of energies, signaling the completion of a cycle and the potential for deep transformations. The power of the Moon entering Scorpio adds an extra layer of depth and passion to your experiences. It invites you to explore your innermost desires, uncover hidden truths, and embrace the transformative power of vulnerability.

APRIL

14 Monday

The current moment is perfectly aligned for charting new goals that expand your horizons, ushering in a positive transformation. As you meticulously design the blueprint of your life, you set in motion a series of events that promise progress and alignment with your desired outcomes. Armed with a fresh attitude and bolstered confidence, you're poised to step out and embark on a journey that offers ample room to revolutionize your world's potential.

15 Tuesday

The wheels of fortune are turning in your favor as news arrives, ushering in a fresh start and unveiling opportunities quietly circulating in the background. This newfound wellspring of possibilities opens doors to an enterprising phase of discovery. Delving into these leads promises advancement as you explore a side avenue that nurtures creativity and brings rising prospects to light. Engaging in innovative enterprises allows your skills to evolve and flourish.

16 Wednesday

As the Moon enters Sagittarius, you may feel a sense of expansion and freedom within your emotional landscape. Sagittarius's fiery and adventurous energy encourages you to seek new experiences, broaden your horizons, and embrace a more optimistic outlook. Simultaneously, Mercury's ingress into Aries makes your thoughts and communication style assertive and direct. You may express your ideas enthusiastically and passionately, eager to take on challenges.

17 Thursday

Mercury's conjunction with Neptune immerses your mind in imagination and intuition. Your thoughts may become dreamy and poetic as Neptune's influence blurs the boundaries between reality and fantasy. It's a time when your communication style becomes more intuitive and compassionate, allowing you to connect with others on a deeper level. Your creativity heightens, and you may draw artistic pursuits or spiritual exploration.

APRIL

18 Friday

As Mars enters Leo, your energy infuses with a fiery passion and a desire for self-expression. You feel a surge of confidence and assertiveness, ready to pursue your goals with boldness and enthusiasm. Your actions become more purposeful and driven as you strive to make your mark and shine in your endeavors. This Mars transit ignites your creative spark and encourages you to take center stage, embracing your individuality and showcasing your talents.

19 Saturday

As the Sun enters the earthy sign of Taurus, you infuse with a grounded and practical energy. It is a time to focus on stability, material comfort, and the sensual pleasures of life. Meanwhile, the harmonious trine between Mars and Neptune adds a touch of inspiration and imagination to your actions. A gentle yet powerful flow of energy supports your dreams and aspirations, allowing you to pursue your goals with compassion and intuition.

20 Sunday

On this Easter Sunday, a day of celebration and rebirth, the cosmos aligns to infuse your life with excitement and transformation. Venus sextile Uranus sparks a spirit of adventure and encourages you to embrace spontaneity in your relationships and creative endeavors. It's a time to break free from the ordinary and explore new possibilities. Meanwhile, Mercury sextile Pluto deepens your understanding and enhances your communication skills.

APRIL

21 Monday

As the Sun squares Mars, you may find yourself experiencing a surge of assertiveness and a desire to take action. However, it's essential to be mindful of potential conflicts or confrontations during this time. Your energy and drive heighten. Avoid impulsive reactions or engaging in unnecessary power struggles. Instead, focus on harnessing this fiery energy to overcome challenges and pursue your goals with determination and resilience.

22 Tuesday

A new project emerges, beckoning you to leave your personal touch upon it. The tide of artistic expression and creativity is rising, paving pathways that accentuate your talents. A significant assignment boosts your spirits, forging a clear path forward for your abilities to shine. By harnessing your capabilities and venturing into new areas of life, you set the stage for favorable outcomes, guided by a chapter of exploration and movement.

23 Wednesday

As the Moon ingresses Pisces and forms a challenging square with Pluto, you may navigate intense emotional depths and transformative energies. This cosmic alignment can stir up deep emotions and unconscious patterns, inviting you to explore the shadows within your psyche. The intensity of this aspect can bring forth power struggles, control issues, or hidden emotions that demand your attention.

24 Thursday

A refreshing change of pace is on the horizon, promising a surge of momentum in your social life. It signals an expansion that will introduce new faces into your world, enriching your circle of friends. This shift propels you toward a more vibrant environment where networking and mingling become the norm. This peachy backdrop connects you with rising possibilities that promise exciting times.

APRIL

25 Friday

As Venus aligns with Saturn, you may feel a sense of seriousness and responsibility in love, relationships, and finances. This conjunction invites you to evaluate your partnerships' long-term stability and commitment. It's a time to assess the value and practicality of your connections and make adjustments. Meanwhile, with the Moon moving into Aries, you may experience a surge of energy and assertiveness. This lunar ingress encourages decisive action.

26 Saturday

An upcoming social gathering emerges as a delightful focal point on your horizon. It promises a beautiful occasion filled with the chance to unwind and connect with others. Sharing precious moments with friends lights the path forward, expanding your social tapestry. This event unveils an avenue for positive change as exciting news arrives to provide a much-needed boost. The wheels are turning, infusing fresh possibilities into your surroundings.

27 Sunday

You may be between personal power and intense emotions with Mars opposing Pluto. This aspect can bring forth fierce conflicts and power struggles, both internally and externally. It's crucial to be mindful of how you channel your energy during this time, as it can lead to destructive or transformative outcomes. The Moon's ingress into Taurus adds a stabilizing influence to the mix, grounding your emotions and encouraging a focus on practicality and stability.

MAY

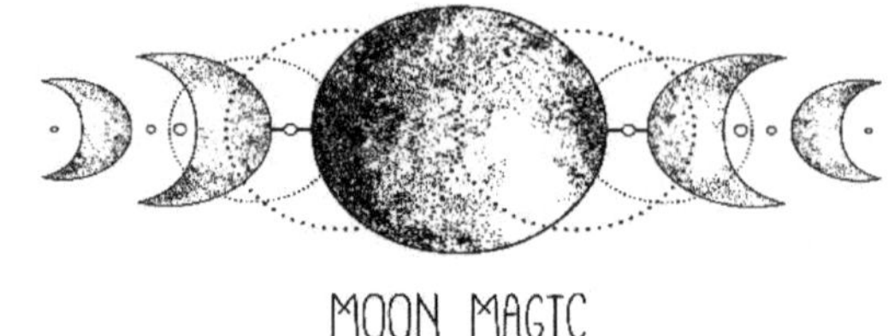

Sun	Mon	Tue	Wed	Thu	Fri	Sat
				1	2	3
4	5	6	7	8	9	10
11	12	13	14	15	16	17
18	19	20	21	22	23	24
25	26	27	28	29	30	31

New Moon

FLOWER MOON

April/May

28 Monday

Set high standards for yourself, and let them be your compass as you navigate towards pleasing prospects in life. Invest your time and energy in situations that bring happiness, and never settle for anything less than you truly deserve. It is your time to shine as you illuminate a path filled with well-being, harmony, and the discovery of hidden gems within your reach. Soon, you'll find yourself attracting opportunities that align perfectly with your vision for future expansion.

29 Tuesday

As the Moon enters Gemini, you may embrace a more curious and adaptable mindset. Your thoughts and emotions may become more fluid, allowing you to engage with the world around you in a versatile and intellectually stimulating way. Gemini's influence encourages you to seek new experiences, expand your knowledge, and connect with others through meaningful conversations. It's a time to embrace your natural curiosity and explore different perspectives.

30 Wednesday

As Venus enters Aries, you may feel a surge of passion and assertiveness in your relationships and personal desires. This fiery energy ignites your sense of self-worth and drives you to pursue your desires with courage and determination. You'll likely feel confident and independent in love and attraction, embracing a more direct and assertive approach. You may be drawn to exciting and adventurous experiences, seeking relationships that challenge and inspire you.

1 Thursday

As the Moon ingresses into Cancer, you may notice a shift in your emotional landscape. Cancer, a water sign, brings nurturing and intuitive energy to your inner world. You may find yourself more attuned to your emotions and those of others, seeking comfort and security in family spaces and connections. You may feel a stronger desire for emotional closeness and a more profound sense of belonging. Allow a retreat into an environment supporting emotional well-being.

May

2 Friday

When Venus aligns with Neptune in conjunction, you are immersed in a world of beauty, romance, and heightened sensitivity. This celestial combination invites you to explore the depths of your imagination and connect with the ethereal realms of love and creativity. You seek to express emotions through forms of creative expression. Your heart becomes open and receptive to the subtle nuances of love and compassion, allowing you to experience empathy and understanding.

3 Saturday

Moon ingress Leo. Use this lunar influence to express your individuality, share your gifts, and lead with a sense of warmth and generosity. Allow your inner radiance to illuminate your path and inspire others to do the same. Remember to listen to your heart's desires and follow your creative impulses, vital to your personal growth and fulfillment. Embrace the Moon's journey through Leo and let your inner lion roar confidently and authentically.

4 Sunday

When Pluto turns retrograde, you may embark on a journey of profound inner transformation. This cosmic event encourages you to delve into the hidden aspects of your psyche, examining your fears, desires, and personal power. It's a time for introspection and self-reflection as you explore the depths of your subconscious mind. You may uncover hidden patterns and unconscious motivations influencing your thoughts, actions, and relationships.

MAY

5 Monday

When Mercury sextiles Jupiter, it opens a gateway to expanded thinking and intellectual growth. This harmonious aspect encourages you to embrace new ideas, broaden your horizons, and engage in meaningful conversations that stimulate your mind. You draw learning, studying, or exploring subjects that pique your curiosity and ignite passion. Your communication skills are enhanced, allowing you to express your thoughts and ideas with clarity and enthusiasm.

6 Tuesday

When Venus forms a sextile aspect with Pluto, you may experience deepening your relationships and a heightened sense of passion and intensity. This aspect brings transformative energy to your connections, allowing for profound emotional experiences and a greater understanding of your desires and needs. You might find yourself drawn to intense and meaningful relationships, seeking depth and authenticity in your interactions.

7 Wednesday

Exciting tidings are on the brink of arriving, casting a sweet and delectable flavor over your life. They herald a beautiful journey of enhanced circumstances intricately woven into the tapestry of your life's expansion. And in a delightful twist of fate, someone from your past reemerges, carrying news and a chance for heartfelt reunions. This unexpected turn of events paints a bright and interconnected future, leaving you feeling deeply supported and content.

8 Thursday

You may find yourself drawn to social activities, seeking the company of friends and loved ones. Embrace the Moon's influence in Libra by cultivating empathy, practicing active listening, and promoting harmony in your interactions. Trust your intuition and let your inner peace guide your decisions and actions. Allow the gentle energy of the Moon in Libra to guide you in creating a balanced and harmonious environment within yourself and your relationships with others.

May

9 Friday

A forthcoming social aspect signals the beginning of a chapter that renews and rejuvenates your energy. It lays the groundwork for stability and equilibrium in your home life, providing a comforting sense of security. Embracing the basics and cherishing quality time with friends acts as a soothing balm, ushering in a theme of improved circumstances and treasured moments. This phase promises self-expression, joy, and delightful encounters with kindred spirits.

10 Saturday

As Mercury moves into Taurus and the Moon enters Scorpio, you may experience a shift in your thought processes and emotional landscape. With Mercury in Taurus, your thinking becomes grounded and practical, focused on taking a deliberate approach to communication. This energy encourages you to think before you speak and express yourself thoughtfully. Meanwhile, with the Moon in Scorpio, your emotions deepen, and you feel like probing beneath the surface.

11 Sunday

You're about to embark on an engaging chapter filled with mingling opportunities. Building rapport with those who resonate with you nurtures harmony, fostering growth and progress within your social life and deepening your connection with the world around you. A celestial luck is at play as the universe orchestrates a symphony of synchronicities just for you. It's as if the stars are conspiring to lead you to the people, places, and experiences that will ignite your soul's passions.

May

12 Monday

During the Full Moon, the energies heighten, and emotions surface. This particular Full Moon is accompanied by a challenging aspect as Mercury squares Pluto, creating a dynamic tension between communication and power dynamics. You may experience intense, transformative conversations that delve into hidden truths. Be mindful of power struggles and manipulative tendencies that may arise during this time.

13 Tuesday

The energy of Sagittarius Moon encourages you to embrace a broader perspective and to be open-minded in your interactions and beliefs. It's a time to seek truth and meaning, engage in philosophical discussions, and embark on journeys of both the physical and metaphorical kind. Allow yourself to embrace the spirit of adventure and let your enthusiasm guide you toward new opportunities and insights.

14 Wednesday

Picture the cosmos as your life's compass and personal motivator. The celestial energies align to boost your determination and grit. Your life becomes a stage for personal growth and meaningful connections. Embrace the cosmic inspiration, and watch as your overall life becomes a testament to your strength and resilience. Life unfolds with heavenly wisdom and inspiration, dear reader. The universe is your guiding light, illuminating the path to personal growth and fulfillment.

15 Thursday

As the Moon moves into Capricorn, you may notice a shift towards a more practical and disciplined approach to your emotions and actions. You will likely become more focused on your goals and responsibilities, seeking stability and structure. It is when you may feel a strong need to be productive and progress in your endeavors. Your determination and perseverance heighten, allowing you to tackle challenges with a systematic and organized mindset.

16 Friday

It's as though the universe has laid out a banquet of shared experiences before you. Your weekend becomes a symphony of laughter, love, and friendship, with each note representing the beauty of human connection. Embrace the cosmic companionship, and watch as your social life thrives. The celestial energies align to boost your magnetism and charisma. Your weekend life becomes a stage for joyful gatherings and heartwarming interactions.

17 Saturday

As the Sun aligns with Uranus, you may experience electrifying energy and a desire for personal freedom and individuality. This planetary aspect can bring sudden and unexpected changes, shaking up routines and prompting you to break free from old patterns. You might find yourself embracing your uniqueness, expressing your authentic self, and pursuing unconventional paths. It is a time to embrace innovation, embrace new ideas, and step outside your comfort zone.

18 Sunday

When Mercury squares Mars, it can create dynamic and potentially challenging energy in your communication and actions. You may feel a strong urge to express your thoughts and ideas, but there can be a tendency towards impulsive or aggressive communication. Be mindful of your words and actions, as conflicts and misunderstandings can arise more easily. However, this aspect also brings a surge of mental energy and motivation to channel into productive endeavors.

May

19 Monday

As you diligently pursue your goals, you gain deeper insights into the broader spectrum of opportunities enveloping your life. This newfound understanding unlocks the code for a meaningful and well-structured journey ahead. By prioritizing stability and equilibrium, you pave the way for enhanced well-being and happiness. You stand at the precipice of closing the chapter on hardship and embracing a lighter, more joyful path.

20 Tuesday

When the Sun forms a harmonious sextile aspect with Saturn, it brings a sense of stability and discipline to your life. This alignment encourages you to take practical steps toward your goals, showing a responsible and structured approach. You may feel a stronger sense of determination and focus, enabling you to make steady progress in your endeavors. The Moon's ingress into Pisces adds a touch of sensitivity and intuition to your emotional landscape.

21 Wednesday

As exciting news arrives, your rhythm and pace find their harmonious groove, paving the way for an enterprising endeavor brimming with potential. These ventures align you with like-minded individuals who share your passions, weaving a fabric of companionship and compatibility into your expanding circle of friends. These beautiful changes unfold against an engaging backdrop, infusing happiness into your world and drawing unique personalities into your orbit.

22 Thursday

When Venus forms a harmonious trine with Mars, it ignites a passionate and rhythmic energy within you. You may feel a desire for love, connection, and creative expression. This aspect enhances your magnetism and charm, making attracting your romantic and imaginative interests easier. Your actions align with desires, and you enthusiastically approach relationships and creative endeavors. Meanwhile, the Sun's sextile with Neptune brings magic and inspiration.

MAY

23 Friday

A celestial symphony is underway, and you are the conductor of your destiny. The cosmic notes dance harmoniously, beckoning you to compose a future filled with melody and meaning. As you lead this cosmic orchestra, be open to the unexpected, for it is in the pauses and crescendos that you'll discover the magic of your potential. The universe has a grand plan for you, unfolding beautifully and unexpectedly.

24 Saturday

When the Sun forms a harmonious trine aspect with Pluto, it empowers you to tap into your inner strength, personal transformation, and the ability to make significant changes in your life. This aspect encourages you to embrace your power and assert yourself in a way that aligns with your authentic self. With the Moon entering Taurus, you may feel grounded and stable. The presence of Mercury conjunct Uranus sparks intellectual brilliance and innovative thinking.

25 Sunday

As Saturn moves into the sign of Aries, you may feel a shift in your approach to discipline, responsibility, and long-term goals. Aries is a fiery and action-oriented sign known for its boldness and assertiveness. With Saturn's influence in Aries, you can take charge of your ambitions and channel your energy into focused, disciplined efforts. This transit encourages you to set clear boundaries, take on leadership roles, and cultivate self-discipline.

26 Monday

Mercury ingress Gemini transit enhances your communication skills and intellectual abilities, allowing you to express yourself easily. With Mercury forming a harmonious sextile with Saturn, you find a balance between your thoughts and practicality. You can effectively apply your ideas and knowledge in a structured and disciplined manner. The Moon's ingress into Gemini further enhances your mental curiosity, encouraging you to interact socially.

27 Tuesday

During the New Moon phase, you experience a potent moment of fresh beginnings and powerful transformation. It is a time of setting intentions and embarking on a new chapter. With Mercury trine Pluto, your communication and thought processes offer depth and intensity. You possess a keen perception and the ability to uncover hidden truths. This aspect empowers you to engage in deep conversations, research, and self-reflection, leading to profound insights.

28 Wednesday

You may be drawn towards a nurturing and comforting atmosphere as the Moon enters Cancer. This lunar shift invites you to tune into your emotions and deeply connect with your inner world. You may feel a greater need for security and seek solace in your life's familiar and cozy spaces. It's a time to prioritize self-care and surround yourself with the people and environments that make you feel safe and supported.

29 Thursday

The planetary energies align to inspire diligence and focus. Your life becomes a canvas for productivity and achievement, where your efforts yield tangible rewards. Embrace this celestial mentorship and watch as your professional and academic pursuits flourish. Your work and studies take center stage as if the cosmic stage is set for your brilliance to shine. Embrace the cosmic support, and watch as your professional and academic life thrives.

June

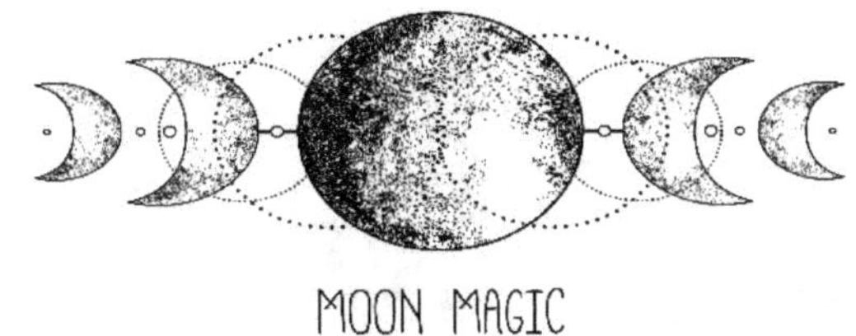

Sun	Mon	Tue	Wed	Thu	Fri	Sat
1	2	3	4	5	6	7
8	9	10	11	12	13	14
15	16	17	18	19	20	21
22	23	24	25	26	27	28
29	30					

NEW MOON

STRAWBERRY MOON

30 Friday

As the Sun and Mercury align, your thoughts and self-expression infuse with vitality and clarity. Your mind is sharp, and you can naturally articulate your ideas confidently. This harmonious energy, complemented by the Moon's ingress into Leo, ignites your passion and creativity. You radiate a magnetic presence and may find yourself drawn to activities that allow you to shine and express your unique personality.

31 Saturday

An intriguing assignment on the horizon illuminates pathways paved with creativity and artistic expression, allowing you to share your gifts with a broader audience. This venture leads you to a vibrant group environment teeming with fresh possibilities. Engaging with kindred spirits becomes second nature, and as communication flows freely, you'll find yourself surrounded by individuals who resonate with your frequency.

1 Sunday

A forthcoming social aspect marks the beginning of a chapter that renews and rejuvenates your energy. It lays the foundation for stability and balance in your home life, providing security. Returning to the basics and spending quality time with friends is a stress reducer, ushering in a theme of enhanced circumstances and cherished moments. This phase promises self-expression, joy, and delightful encounters with kindred spirits.

JUNE

2 Monday

As the Moon moves into Virgo, you may find yourself shifting your focus towards practical matters and a sense of organization. You can pay attention to the details and engage in productive tasks. You feel efficient and seek to streamline routines. Use this energy to analyze and improve your daily life, whether it's through decluttering, setting goals, or enhancing your productivity. Your attention to detail serves you well during this lunar phase.

3 Tuesday

Grounded energy permeates your environment, signifying a time of significant improvement. It empowers you to turn the corner and reveal a brighter future through strategic planning and project development, showing tremendous promise and connecting you to positive change. By investing time in designing plans and nurturing projects, you build upon your talents and progress confidently toward great success.

4 Wednesday

As the Moon enters Libra, you may notice a heightened focus on balance, harmony, and relationships. This transit is a time to seek unity in your interactions with others, striving for fairness and cooperation. You may feel a greater need for social connection and a desire to engage in activities that promote beauty, art, and aesthetic pleasure. Your sense of diplomacy and fairness can be a valuable asset in resolving conflicts and fostering healthy relationships.

5 Thursday

Venus sextiles Jupiter; it brings harmonious and expansive energy to your relationships and experiences. This aspect encourages you to embrace joy, abundance, and positivity in your interactions with others. It fosters a sense of optimism and optimism, inspiring you to pursue opportunities for growth, adventure, and connection. Your social life may flourish as you attract opportunities for fun, romance, and enjoyable experiences.

JUNE

6 Friday

You may find yourself drawn to activities that engage your senses, such as indulging in delicious food, enjoying nature, or surrounding yourself with art and music that uplifts your spirit. It's a time to nurture your relationships with love and care. Venus in Taurus invites you to slow down, savor the present moment, and create a more harmonious and abundant environment. It's a favorable period for cultivating stability and enjoying the simple pleasures that bring you joy.

7 Saturday

It's a time to embrace your power and confront any shadows or hidden aspects of yourself. The Moon in Scorpio encourages you to trust your instincts and follow your intuition, even if it means exploring the darker corners of your soul. It is a transformative period where you have the opportunity to release emotional baggage and emerge stronger and wiser. Allow yourself to embrace vulnerability and emotional depth, which can lead to profound personal growth and healing.

8 Sunday

When Mercury conjuncts Jupiter, you can expect a boost in your mental faculties and an expansion of your perspective. This alignment enhances your ability to think big and see the bigger picture in various areas of your life. It encourages you to broaden your knowledge, engage in stimulating conversations, and seek wisdom from different sources. With Mercury's ingress into Cancer, your thoughts and communication take on a more emotional and nurturing tone.

JUNE

9 Monday

When Mercury squares Saturn, you may experience a temporary clash between your thoughts and responsibilities. It can feel challenging to express yourself or convey your ideas effectively. With the Moon's ingress into Sagittarius, your emotions may bring a desire for freedom. You might feel more optimistic and open-minded, ready to explore new possibilities. Be mindful of the square between Venus and Pluto, as it may intensify your relationships and financial matters.

10 Tuesday

As you diligently work on your goals, you gain a deeper understanding of the broader picture of opportunities surrounding your life. This insight unlocks the code for a meaningful and well-designed journey ahead. Focusing on stability and balance paves the way for enhanced well-being and happiness. You are on the brink of closing the chapter on hardship and embracing a lighter, more joyful path, with exciting news poised to give you an unexpected boost.

11 Wednesday

Embrace the energy of the Full Moon to bring clarity to your emotions and strengthen the bonds with your loved ones. It's a time of synergy and alignment between your mind and heart, allowing you to express yourself authentically and experience more profound connections. Trust in the transformative power of this celestial dance and let it guide you towards greater love and fulfillment in your relationships.

12 Thursday

When the Moon ingresses Capricorn, there is a shift towards more grounded and practical energy in your life. You may feel a sense of increased discipline, focus, and a desire to achieve your goals and responsibilities. This planetary aspect is a time to channel your determination and work towards creating a solid foundation for your ambitions. You may take a more structured and organized approach to your tasks, prioritizing efficiency and long-term success.

13 Friday

As you embark on a journey of developing your life, exciting news is set to arrive, drawing anticipation and unveiling a path worth savoring. The wheel of fortune is turning in your favor, ushering in heightened security and a more profound sense of meaning; engaging in lively and thoughtful discussions ushers in improvements in your social sphere, offering a meaningful path that awaits your embrace.

14 Saturday

When the Moon enters Aquarius, you may experience a shift in your emotional landscape towards a more independent and progressive outlook. Aquarius energy encourages you to embrace your uniqueness and think outside the box. It's a time to connect with your inner rebel and explore innovative ideas and alternative perspectives. You may feel detached and objective, allowing you to see situations from a broader viewpoint.

15 Sunday

Mars square Uranus aspect can bring about sudden and unexpected events or disruptions that require you to adapt and think on your feet. It's important to channel this energy in productive and constructive ways rather than allowing it to lead to impulsive or reckless actions. Meanwhile, Jupiter square Saturn presents a dynamic tension between expansion and restriction. You may feel torn between pursuing your ambitions and facing practical limitations or responsibilities.

JUNE

16 Monday

When the Moon enters Pisces, you may find yourself in a more reflective and emotionally sensitive state. Pisces is a sign associated with intuition, empathy, and imagination. You might feel more attuned to your emotions and the subtle energies around you during this time. It's a favorable period for self-reflection, meditation, and creative activities. You may also feel a deeper connection with others and a heightened sense of compassion and empathy.

17 Tuesday

When Mars ingresses Virgo, you experience a shift towards more practical and detail-oriented energy. Virgo is an earth sign known for its analytical and meticulous nature. You may be motivated to tackle tasks precisely and efficiently during this time. You focus on organization, productivity, and improving your daily routines. It's a significant period to take a proactive approach to your health and well-being, paying attention to nutrition, exercise, and self-care.

18 Wednesday

When the Moon ingress Aries, you experience a renewed energy surge and enthusiasm. Aries is a fiery sign known for its assertiveness, courage, and passion. During this time, you may desire to take action, initiate new projects, and assert yourself in various areas of your life. Your confidence and self-motivation heighten, empowering you to pursue your goals with determination. Allow the fiery energy of Aries to fuel your passions and drive you toward success.

19 Thursday

When Jupiter squares Neptune, you may face a clash between idealism and reality. This aspect can bring disillusionment or confusion as your expectations clash with the circumstances. It's essential to be cautious of over-idealizing situations or people, as this can lead to disappointment. Suppose you are choosing different paths; it's a time to reflect on your beliefs, dreams, and aspirations and assess whether they align with life's practical realities.

June

20 Friday

Brightening Horizons: Your life radiates with newfound brightness as you embark on expanding your horizons. This journey combines refreshing potential and happy changes that connect you with supportive friends and engaging discussions. A unique cycle unfolds, ushering in a wave of invitations for your social life, offering an upgrade and the opportunity to expand your circle of friends. Life unfolds in a delightful flavor, offering a journey worth savoring.

21 Saturday

As the Moon moves into Taurus and the Sun enters Cancer, you can embrace the energy of stability, nurturing, and emotional connection. The June Solstice marks a turning point, where the days grow shorter or longer, depending on your hemisphere. It's a time to honor the cycles of nature and find balance within yourself. You may need comfort, security, and sensual pleasures with the Moon in Taurus.

22 Sunday

With Mars forming a harmonious sextile to Jupiter and the Sun in a challenging square with Saturn, you navigate a dynamic blend of energies. The Mars-Jupiter sextile infuses you with confidence, motivation, and enthusiasm. It encourages you to take bold actions, expand your horizons, and embrace opportunities for growth and success. However, the Sun's square with Saturn brings a dose of reality and highlights areas where you may encounter obstacles or limitations.

23 Monday

With the Moon moving into Gemini, there is a shift in your emotional landscape, encouraging curiosity, adaptability, and a desire for mental stimulation. You may find yourself seeking variety and engaging in diverse interests and conversations. However, the Sun's square aspect of Neptune brings a subtle challenge, blurring the boundaries between reality and fantasy. This cosmic tension can create confusion, illusions, and a sense of uncertainty.

24 Tuesday

With the Sun and Jupiter coming together in conjunction, you infuse with optimism and abundance. This celestial alignment boosts confidence and a heightened belief in your potential. You may desire to explore new horizons, take risks, and embrace growth opportunities. Your energy is expansive and enthusiastic, attracting positive experiences and connections. You can embrace your inner potential, set ambitious goals, and passionately pursue your dreams.

25 Wednesday

With the Moon entering Cancer and the arrival of a New Moon, you are being called to nurture your emotional well-being and create a fresh start. This lunar phase presents an opportunity for introspection, reflection, and setting intentions. It is a time to connect with your inner self and honor your feelings. The New Moon in Cancer invites you to listen to your intuition and tap into your emotional intelligence as you embark on self-discovery and transformation.

26 Thursday

With Mercury forming a sextile with Uranus and the Sun forming a sextile with Mars, electric and dynamic energy in the air encourages you to embrace your uniqueness and confidently express yourself. Mercury's ingress into Leo further enhances your communication skills and enables you to speak your truth passionately and authentically. Your ideas and thoughts can flow effortlessly, and you can think outside the box and develop innovative solutions.

27 Friday

Embrace self-expression, whether it be through art, communication, or any form of creative endeavor that brings you joy. Allow your inner fire to fuel your enthusiasm and ignite a sense of purpose. Embrace your natural leadership qualities and take charge of your life with courage and determination. Let the Moon in Leo remind you of your inherent worth and the power you hold within. Express your authenticity and let your true self shine in all its glory.

28 Saturday

With Mercury forming harmonious trines to Saturn and Neptune, you find yourself in a period of enhanced mental clarity and intuition. Your mind is sharp, focused, and capable of great depth. You have solid knowledge and experience that allows you to approach tasks and challenges confidently and precisely. Your ability to think logically and practically is supported by Saturn's influence, while Neptune brings a touch of inspiration and imagination to your thoughts and ideas.

29 Sunday

When Mercury opposes Pluto, and the Moon moves into Virgo, you may experience a heightened intensity in your thoughts and emotions. This alignment brings profound probing energy to your mental processes, urging you to delve into the depths of your mind and uncover hidden truths. Your thoughts may become more analytical and critical as you seek to unravel mysteries and gain a deeper understanding of the world around you.

July

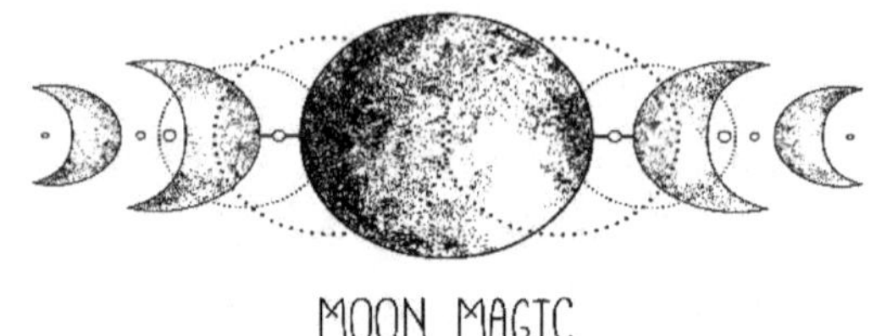

Sun	Mon	Tue	Wed	Thu	Fri	Sat
		1	2	3	4	5
6	7	8	9	10	11	12
13	14	15	16	17	18	19
20	21	22	23	24	25	26
27	28	29	30	31		

ARIES

New Moon

Buck Moon

JUNE/JULY

30 Monday

By placing your life as the top priority, you open the door to new growth pathways, each brimming with the essence of inspiration. This decision introduces a social dimension, propelling you into an enriching environment where animated conversations and meaningful connections thrive. Before long, you'll naturally attract opportunities that seamlessly align with your vision for future expansion. A new cycle takes center stage, propelling your life to unprecedented heights.

1 Tuesday

When the Moon enters Libra, you seek harmony, balance, and cooperation in your relationships and surroundings. You have an awareness of the needs and perspectives of others, and you strive to find common ground and compromise. This lunar influence brings a sense of fairness and justice, and you may find yourself mediating conflicts or seeking peaceful resolutions. Your focus shifts towards creating harmonious environments and fostering positive connections.

2 Wednesday

Official recognition illuminates the path to increased opportunities, bringing your talents to a broader audience. Ahead lie options that allow you to reshape your goals and initiate transformative changes. Advancement is on the horizon, ushering in new projects and creative adventures, setting the stage for growth and expansion. It kindles fresh artistic projects and endeavors, aligning your efforts with higher success.

3 Thursday

Exploring the uncharted potential on the periphery of your environment unveils pathways rich in connection and support. This discovery brings personal development to the forefront, and as you make significant strides in improving your life, you forge a winning trajectory. A new realm of possibilities beckons you forward, infusing harmony into your life. These changes clear the fog and enhance your life, building grounded foundations that promote balance and stability.

JULY

4 Friday

When the Moon enters Scorpio, you can dive deep into the depths of your emotions and explore the hidden realms of your psyche. This astrological transit brings intensity, passion, and a desire for transformation. You may find yourself craving authenticity and seeking profound connections with others. The Scorpio Moon encourages you to confront your fears, embrace your vulnerabilities, and let go of what no longer serves. It's a time of emotional regeneration and rebirth.

5 Saturday

News on the horizon promises greater involvement in your social life, initiating a bustling phase of dream development and goal design. As you nurture your life, you move toward a socially connected era that offers support and camaraderie. This favorable environment is ideal for cultivating new hobbies and engaging with like-minded individuals. The wheels are in motion as you head toward rising prospects.

6 Sunday

Venus forms a sextile with Saturn, bringing a harmonious blend of stability and creativity to your relationships and personal values. This aspect supports you in building solid foundations and connections based on mutual respect. It encourages you to find a balance between practicality and romanticism, allowing you to appreciate the beauty and depth of your relationships. As Venus also forms a sextile with Neptune, inspiration infuses your interactions and endeavors.

JULY

7 Monday

When Uranus enters Gemini, it brings fresh and innovative energy into your life. This transit encourages you to embrace change, explore new ideas, and express your individuality in unique and exciting ways. Your mind becomes open to unconventional perspectives, and you seek progressive and forward-thinking pursuits. With Venus forming a trine with Pluto, there is a potent blend of passion and transformation in your relationships and personal values.

8 Tuesday

Remaining authentic to your inner self unlocks a path of profound growth, resonating with the person you are becoming. Life's pace quickens, fostering a productive environment that encourages progress. Enhanced stability and security form the bedrock for balanced foundations, and by embracing this chapter, you expand horizons and welcome new possibilities. A gateway emerges, streamlining your progress and fostering success in your world.

9 Wednesday

With the Moon moving into Capricorn, you are entering a phase of practicality, responsibility, and ambition. This lunar transit encourages you to focus on your goals and take a structured approach to your emotions and daily tasks. You may feel a more substantial need for stability and a desire to establish solid foundations in various areas of your life. Use this time to plan, organize, prioritize responsibilities, and cultivate discipline and determination.

10 Thursday

During a Full Moon, you may experience heightened emotions and energy. It is a time of culmination and completion, where the intentions and efforts you have put into motion reach their peak. This transit is an opportunity for reflection, evaluation, and release. You may seek clarity and illumination in different areas of your life. Please pay attention to your emotions and inner wisdom as they guide you toward what needs to be acknowledged and let go of.

July

11 Friday

When the Moon enters Aquarius, you may experience a shift in your emotional energy. Aquarius is an air sign known for its independent and innovative nature. You may feel a greater desire for freedom, exploration, and intellectual stimulation during this time. You may find yourself drawn to unconventional ideas, social causes, and a sense of community—time to connect with like-minded individuals, engage in group activities, and broaden your perspectives.

12 Saturday

Life's tapestry is about to be woven with the vibrant threads of a social gathering on the horizon. It's a captivating focal point, promising relaxation and cherished connections. As you share moments with friends, your path is illuminated, expanding your social world. This event signifies a positive turning point, as exciting news is set to breeze into your surroundings, infusing them with fresh energy.

13 Sunday

When Saturn turns retrograde, you can reflect on your responsibilities, boundaries, and long-term goals. It is time for introspection and inner work as you reassess the structures and limitations in your life. You may crave solitude and self-reflection as you dive deep into your emotions and subconscious patterns. The Moon's ingress into Pisces adds a touch of sensitivity and intuition to your emotional landscape, inviting you to connect with your spiritual side.

14 Monday

Life offers a chance to infuse creativity into a new project, igniting the spark of prosperity. This journey propels you into a dynamic realm where you work with your talents and nurture your abilities, breaking through barriers that once hindered progress. The universe supports your expansion, making it an ideal time to chase your dreams. Your willingness to invest energy into your personal growth creates significant improvement, setting the fires of inspiration ablaze.

15 Tuesday

An emphasis on improving your situation draws an inspiring journey into your life. Rising prospects ahead crack the code to expand life outwardly. You discover a new approach that draws momentum into your world, and as the pace of life quickens, you soon feel buoyed by encouraging results. Being proactive helps you gain a foothold in an ambitious and exciting area. It places you on a path of growth and advancement.

16 Wednesday

When the Moon enters Aries, you may experience a surge of energy and motivation. You are infused with confidence and assertiveness, ready to take on new challenges and pursue your goals with vigor. This fiery transit is a time for bold action and initiating projects that excite you. You may feel the urge to assert your individuality and express yourself authentically. Trust your instincts and embrace your inner fire as you navigate the world.

17 Thursday

You are in a time of transition, and this can feel unsettling. It opens up a journey that draws rejuvenation and renewal into your life. Evolving and growing your abilities nurtures your life and offers side journeys to explore. New horizons tempt you forward and carry you on the winds of change. Reawakening to the magic and possibility surrounding your life marks a turning point that draws blessings. An invitation ahead takes you forward on the winds of change.

July

18 Friday

When Mercury turns retrograde, you may experience a period of introspection and reflection. It's a time to slow down, review, and reassess various aspects of your life. As the Moon enters Taurus, you can ground and find stability amidst the shifting energies. This combination invites you to communicate and connect harmoniously with others. The sextile between Mercury and Venus enhances your ability to express feelings and thoughts with grace and diplomacy.

19 Saturday

Your social life is poised to reach new heights, heralding a phase of mingling and harmonious connections with friends. The melodious tunes of music serenade your surroundings as thoughtful conversations become the soundtrack of your happiness. Stepping out into a vibrant community environment feels effortless, and engaging with supportive individuals enriches your life. These delightful changes create space for grounded foundations, ushering in peace and stability.

20 Sunday

When the Moon moves into Gemini, you may feel a surge of intellectual energy and curiosity. Your mind becomes active and agile, craving stimulation and new experiences. It is a time to engage in conversations, gather information, and expand your knowledge. You find yourself drawn to social interactions and connecting with others on an intellectual level. Your communication skills heighten, and you discover expressing your thoughts and ideas more manageable.

21 Monday

Opportunity comes knocking and opens a journey that inspires progress around your life. It captures the essence of wanderlust as you develop a dream that promotes happiness. As you design the path and create progress around your life, you build more balanced foundations that offer heightened security and stability. Life opens to a vibrant landscape that redefines what you thought possible in your world. You are ready to open the floodgates and embrace a brighter chapter.

22 Tuesday

As the Moon moves into Cancer and the Sun enters Leo, you may experience a shift in your emotional landscape and a renewed sense of self-expression. Cancer's nurturing and sensitive energy combines with Leo's bold and confident nature, creating a powerful blend of emotions and self-assurance. During this time, you are encouraged to honor your feelings and seek comfort and security in your personal life.

23 Wednesday

With the Sun's sextile Uranus, there is an exciting energy of innovation and change. This cosmic aspect encourages embracing uniqueness and breaking free from old patterns. It's a time to explore possibilities and step out of your comfort zone. Meanwhile, with Venus square Mars, your relationships may have tension and a need to balance assertiveness and harmony. You can improve relationship dynamics by navigating the dynamic interplay between Venus and Mars.

24 Thursday

With the Sun trine Saturn, you can create stability and structure. This aspect provides a strong foundation for ambitions and goals, allowing you to manifest your desires with discipline. As the Moon ingresses Leo, you enjoy rising confidence, creativity, and self-expression. This lunar energy encourages you to embrace your unique talents and shine your light. Intuition and imagination heighten with the Sun trine Neptune, enabling you to tap into spiritual insights.

July

25 Friday

You may face intense power dynamics and transformative experiences with the Sun opposing Pluto. It can be a time of inner turmoil and personal growth as you dismantle old patterns and beliefs that no longer serve you. You may encounter situations or individuals who challenge your sense of self and force you to confront your shadow side. This opposition can be both unsettling and empowering, pushing you to reclaim your power and transform your life.

26 Saturday

You may find yourself more analytical and critical, seeking efficiency and improvement in your work and personal life. It is an opportunity to be diligent and meticulous in your approach, striving for perfection and seeking ways to serve others. Embracing the energy of the Virgo Moon, you can enhance your productivity, health, and overall sense of stability. Take time to prioritize tasks, establish healthy habits, and refine your skills.

27 Sunday

Exciting revelations await, infusing a delectable sweetness into your life, launching a journey of enhanced circumstances, opening doors to reconnect with your circle of friends, and even rekindling connections with individuals from your past. This unforeseen twist paints a bright future with interconnection, support, and heartfelt contentment. Thoughtful discussions with your circle of friends yield constructive dialogues, shedding light on exciting new options for your life.

28 Monday

The shifting landscape on your life's horizon ignites your passion for pursuing meaningful goals, marking the start of a transformative phase. Opportunities abound, expanding your horizons and offering fresh perspectives. Your new approach propels you toward your goals, energizing your pursuits with purpose. Accelerating life's pace promises exciting results, affirming your ability to succeed in ambitious endeavors.

29 Tuesday

When the Moon enters Libra, you may experience a shift towards seeking balance and harmony in your life. This transit is when you may feel more inclined to focus on your relationships and interactions with others. You may find yourself drawn to socializing, collaborating, and seeking compromise in conflicts. The Libra Moon encourages you to weigh different perspectives and consider the needs of those around you.

30 Wednesday

Your perseverance and willingness to grow your life draw new options into your world. Don't worry too much, as a sign ahead will give you a slipstream of possibility that extends your life in a meaningful direction. An uptick of potential emerges, bringing a chapter brimming with support and caring shared with friends. You spread your wings to embrace a transformation that propels your life outward—fresh adventures beckon, illuminating personal development.

31 Thursday

With Venus entering Cancer, your focus may shift towards creating a nurturing and emotionally supportive environment for yourself and those around you. You may feel more inclined to express your feelings and seek comfort and intimacy in your relationships. This transit can enhance emotional sensitivity and empathy, allowing you to connect with others. As the Moon moves into Scorpio, there may be a desire to explore the depths of your emotions and uncover hidden truths.

AUGUST

Sun	Mon	Tue	Wed	Thu	Fri	Sat
					1	2
3	4	5	6	7	8	9
10	11	12	13	14	15	16
17	18	19	20	21	22	23
24	25	26	27	28	29	30
31 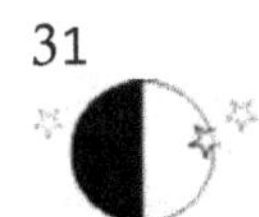						

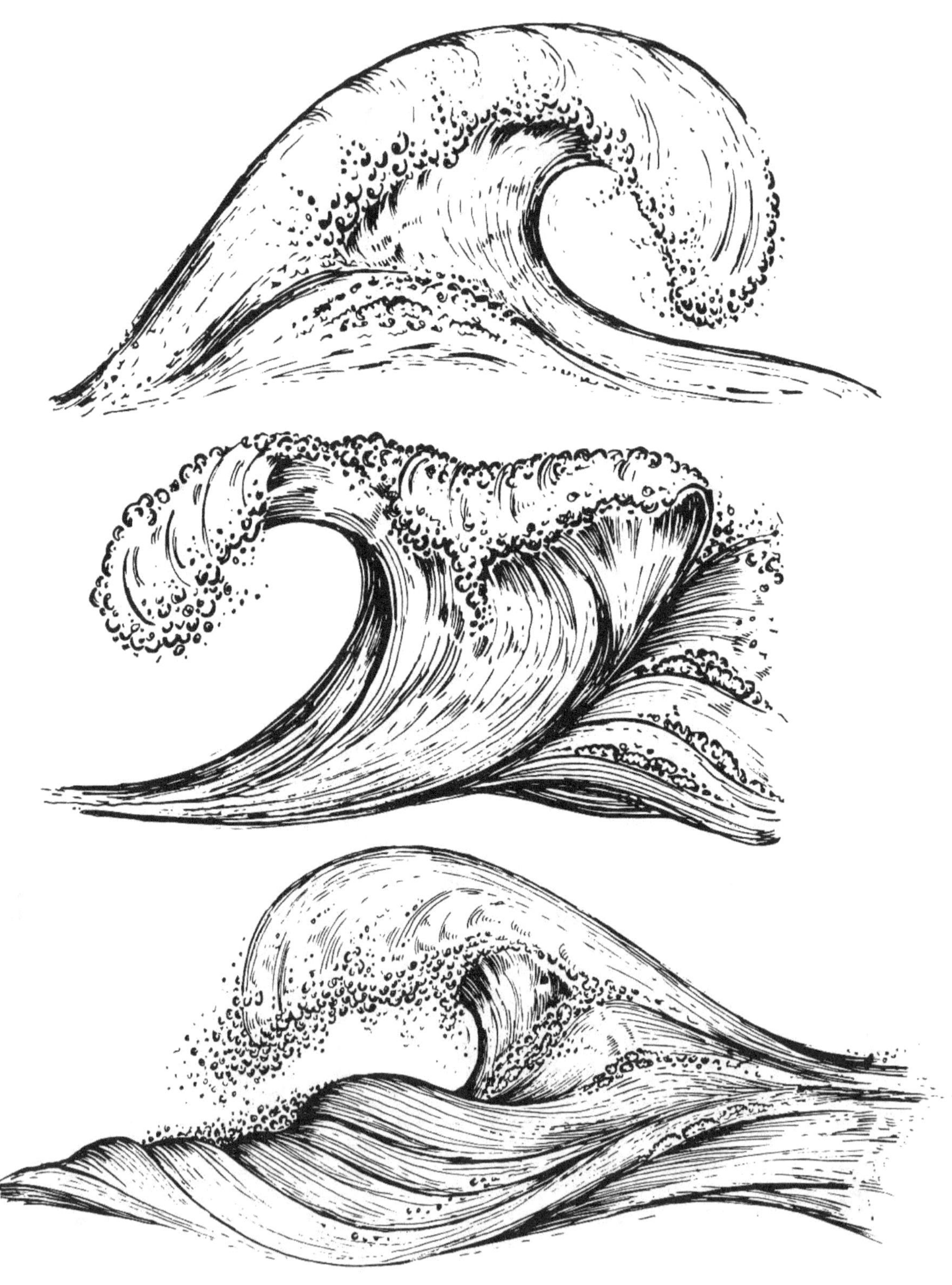

NEW MOON

Sturgeon Moon

August

1 Friday

With Venus forming challenging squares with Saturn and Neptune, you might experience tension and uncertainty in your relationships and personal values. The Venus-Saturn square could bring feelings of restriction or limitation in love and financial matters, causing you to question the stability of certain connections or commitments. At the same time, the Venus-Neptune square may lead to idealizing, making it essential to be cautious in matters of love and trust.

2 Saturday

With beautiful changes on the horizon, you're granted the green light to shift your focus towards personal goals. This cosmic guidance system will steer you toward opportunities you might have never imagined, propelling you toward a future filled with brilliance and purpose. As the celestial gears turn, a transformative energy sweeps through your life like a refreshing breeze. The cosmos is your ally in this metamorphosis, guiding you toward a future with boundless potential.

3 Sunday

As the Moon moves into Sagittarius, you may feel a sense of adventure and optimism entering your life. This placement encourages you to explore new horizons, expand your knowledge, and seek deeper meanings in your experiences. You might crave philosophical discussions, spiritual pursuits, or long-distance travel during this time. Embrace the freedom-loving spirit of Sagittarius as it inspires you to break from routine and embrace new opportunities.

AUGUST

4 Monday

Maintaining a distance from office politics proves to be a wise choice, shielding you from unnecessary drama and preserving your productivity. Focusing on building stable foundations fosters equilibrium in your professional life and initiates a journey teeming with prospects for improvement. The overarching theme of progress acts as a guiding light, unveiling a brighter chapter filled with rewards, change, growth, and triumphant success.

5 Tuesday

As the Moon enters Capricorn, you may notice a shift towards a more disciplined and structured approach to your emotions and actions. This transit encourages you to focus on your long-term goals and take practical steps toward achieving them. You might feel a stronger sense of responsibility and a desire to organize your life more efficiently. Embrace this time to set realistic plans and work diligently towards them.

6 Wednesday

As Mars enters Libra, you may experience a shift in how you handle conflicts and pursue your desires. This transit encourages you to find balance and harmony in your actions, emphasizing the importance of diplomacy and cooperation in your interactions with others. You might feel more inclined to seek compromises and consider the needs and perspectives of those around you. Approach challenges tactfully and create win-win solutions that benefit everyone involved.

7 Thursday

As you detach from drama and surround yourself with supportive individuals, life takes on a lighter, sweeter tone. An air of change sweeps in, creating a dynamic and busy atmosphere filled with news, invitations, and mingling opportunities. Nurturing your social life leads to constructive dialogues and enriching moments with friends who add value to your journey, setting the stage for self-expression and growth.

AUGUST

8 Friday

With the Moon entering Aquarius and Mars forming a trine with Uranus, you may feel the excitement and a desire for change and innovation. This combination encourages you to break free from routine and embrace your individuality. You might find yourself drawn to unique and unconventional ideas, seeking opportunities to express your true self. The harmonious trine between Mars and Uranus empowers you with the confidence to embrace new experiences.

9 Saturday

With Mars forming oppositions to Saturn and Neptune during this Full Moon, you might grapple with conflicting energies and emotions. Mars opposed Saturn can bring frustration and challenges, making it feel like you are hitting roadblocks and encountering resistance in your endeavors. On the other hand, Mars opposed Neptune, which can create a sense of confusion or disillusionment, making it difficult to know which direction to take or what actions to prioritize.

10 Sunday

With the Moon entering Pisces and Mars forming a trine with Pluto, you might experience a time of emotional depth and powerful transformation. The Moon in Pisces encourages introspection, inviting you to connect with your inner self and emotions as you engage in creative pursuits or spiritual practices that nurture your soul. Meanwhile, the harmonious trine between Mars and Pluto empowers you with solid determination and the ability to make significant changes in your life.

AUGUST

11 Monday

As Mercury finally turns direct, you can expect relief and clarity in communication and decision-making. There might have been some misunderstandings or delays during its retrograde period, but now you can move forward with more confidence and direction. Take this time to review any plans or projects you put on hold and make necessary adjustments. You might also find that stalled negotiations or conversations flow more smoothly.

---

12 Tuesday

With Saturn sextile Uranus, you may find a harmonious balance between stability and innovation. This aspect encourages you to embrace positive change while maintaining a solid foundation. It's a time to explore new possibilities and ideas while staying grounded in practicality and responsibility. Additionally, the Venus conjunct Jupiter aspect brings joy, abundance, and optimism to your relationships and experiences.

---

13 Wednesday

Anticipate transformative changes that reignite your creativity and pave the way for growth. An enticing opportunity beckons, inviting you to venture into greener pastures. It heralds a happier phase marked by significant developments in areas that resonate deeply with you. As life picks up speed, a more productive pace drives your potential to flourish, guiding you toward a triumphant transformation journey.

---

14 Thursday

With the Moon's ingress into Taurus, you may notice a sense of stability and grounding in your emotions and actions. This energy fosters a deeper connection to your feelings and a desire for comfort and security. It's a favorable time to indulge in simple pleasures and care for yourself. Your emotions may feel more steady and reliable, and you might find it easier to maintain calm and tranquility. You can enjoy delicious food or engage in peace and contentment activities.

August

15 Friday

With Mercury sextile Mars, you may experience a boost in mental energy and communication skills. This aspect can enhance your ability to express yourself assertively and confidently. Your mind is sharp, and you can effectively communicate your ideas and opinions to others. It's a favorable time for making decisions, initiating conversations, and tackling tasks that require mental focus and determination.

16 Saturday

With the Moon ingress Gemini, you may feel more curious and mentally active. This influence can enhance your communication skills, making connecting with others and engaging in exciting conversations easier. Your mind may buzz with new ideas and possibilities, and you might feel drawn to learning and exploring various topics. It's a great time to be social, as you'll likely enjoy interacting with friends and colleagues.

17 Sunday

You are entering a cycle of increasing possibility. Being open to connecting with friends and sharing lively catch-ups draws a bonus into your social life. It offers a changing scene that nurtures stability and happiness and brings grounded foundations that keep life engaging and vibrant. It brings an ambient environment that fosters harmony through the supportive conversations shared with kindred spirits.

18 Monday

As Mercury forms a harmonious sextile with Mars, you may notice a boost in your communication and mental agility. Ideas and thoughts flow more smoothly, allowing you to articulate your thoughts with confidence and assertiveness. Your assertive nature combined with the Moon's ingress into Cancer brings emotional sensitivity. During this time, you might crave nurturing and caring for yourself and others, seeking comfort and security in your close relationships.

19 Tuesday

Favorable events merge to create a window of opportunity, illuminating your path toward expanding your circle of friends. This journey promises to be supportive and engaging, a chapter you'll hold dear. A forthcoming transition releases outworn energies surrounding your life, opening the door to a new journey. This adventure beckons, ushering in an exhilarating era of freedom, expansion, and growth.

20 Wednesday

As the Moon enters Leo, you'll likely feel a surge of creative and expressive energy. This celestial event brings a sense of playfulness and a desire to shine in the spotlight. Your emotions may heighten, and you might seek validation and recognition for your endeavors. It's a time when you can confidently share your ideas and talents with others, and your natural charisma will draw people toward you.

21 Thursday

News arrives, which brings a boost. It points the way towards a social aspect that brings invitations to mingle. Laying the foundations for improvement in your social life opens your world to new people who radiate your frequency. Lively discussions in a group environment nurture happiness and well-being. The events ahead offer remarkable opportunities for growth and happiness. It speaks of a shift forward that provides you with an open road of possibility.

AUGUST

22 Friday

As the Sun moves into Virgo, you may experience a shift in focus towards practicality, organization, and attention to detail. This period encourages you to analyze and refine your goals, bringing clarity and efficiency to your daily life. Your analytical skills emerge, allowing you to tackle challenges systematically. This transit is an excellent time for self-improvement and setting up healthy routines that enhance your well-being.

23 Saturday

The New Moon signifies a time of introspection and self-reflection, making it an ideal moment to identify areas of your life that require improvement or refinement. Use this lunar energy to plan and strategize carefully, as it can significantly impact the success of your future endeavors. Embrace the analytical and critical thinking nature of the Virgo Moon to make the most of this cycle and set yourself on a path of growth and fulfillment.

24 Sunday

With the Sun forming a challenging square aspect to Uranus, you may feel a surge of unpredictability and restlessness. This alignment can bring unexpected disruptions and sudden changes to your plans and routines. You might find yourself craving more freedom and independence, leading you to rebel against constraints or limitations. It's essential to be open to adapting to the unexpected and embracing a more flexible approach.

AUGUST

25 Monday

With the Moon's ingress into Libra and Venus entering Leo, you may experience a focus on your relationships and personal expression. Libra's influence's harmonious and diplomatic qualities can inspire you to seek balance and harmony in your interactions with others. With Venus in Leo, your desire for attention and affection may increase, and you'll likely feel more inclined to express your unique personality and creativity.

26 Tuesday

With Venus forming harmonious trines to Saturn and Neptune, as well as a sextile to Uranus, you may find yourself experiencing a period of enhanced emotional connections and meaningful experiences in your relationships. The trine with Saturn brings stability and commitment to your romantic partnerships, encouraging you to build a solid foundation based on trust and shared values. The sextile to Uranus adds a spark of excitement to your day.

27 Wednesday

As Venus opposes Pluto, you may encounter intense emotions and power struggles in your relationships and personal desires. This astrological aspect can bring forth feelings of jealousy, possessiveness, and a need for control. You might find yourself grappling with trust and intimacy issues during this time. It's essential to be aware of any manipulative tendencies or destructive behaviors that could arise. Try to delve deeper into the root causes of any emotional conflicts.

28 Thursday

Scorpio's influence brings a deep and mysterious energy, urging you to delve into your innermost feelings and thoughts. You might find yourself seeking meaningful connections and experiences with emotional depth and authenticity. It is a time to embrace your intuitive side and explore the hidden aspects of your psyche. While your emotions might run deep, allow yourself moments of solitude and self-reflection to gain insights into inner conflicts or desires.

AUGUST

29 Friday

Uranus sextile Neptune. This astrological influence encourages you to explore new and unconventional ideas while tapping into your creative and intuitive nature. You may find yourself inspired to break free from old limitations and embrace a more progressive and open-minded approach to various aspects of your life. During this harmonious alignment, your vision for the future may expand, allowing you to dream big and envision possibilities beyond the ordinary.

30 Saturday

Sagittarius Moon's influence brings a desire for physical and intellectual exploration, encouraging you to seek new experiences and broaden your horizons. You might feel a strong urge to break free from routines and embrace spontaneity, allowing yourself to be open to exciting opportunities that come your way. Engage in activities that nurture your sense of freedom and independence, such as travel, learning, or connecting with different cultures and philosophies.

31 Sunday

You are ready to craft your vision and head towards developing your dreams. As you open the book on a new realm of potential for your life, you stir up exciting options worth your time. Developing and designing new goals creates a gateway toward advancement. The shifting scenery on the horizon excites you, inspiring the pursuit of meaningful goals. It marks the onset of a phase of growth that ushers in positive change.

SEPTEMBER

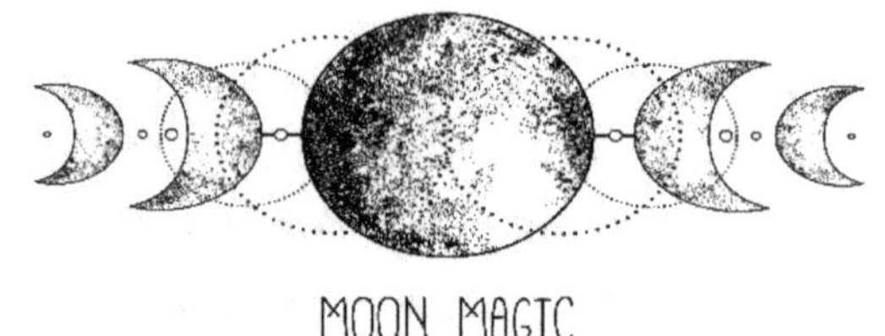

Sun	Mon	Tue	Wed	Thu	Fri	Sat
	1	2	3	4	5	6
7	8	9	10	11	12	13
14	15	16	17	18	19	20
21	22	23	24	25	26	27
28	29	30				

New Moon

CORN/HARVEST MOON

SEPTEMBER

1 Monday

With Saturn's ingress into Pisces, you may notice a subtle yet significant shift in your approach to responsibilities and boundaries. Pisces' influence encourages you to tap into your emotional depths and explore your intuition. You might feel a heightened sense of compassion and empathy towards others, prompting you to extend a helping hand to those in need. Saturn's presence in Pisces invites you to address unresolved emotional issues and work towards healing and closure.

2 Tuesday

The Moon in Capricorn brings a sense of practicality and determination to your feelings, encouraging you to take a more disciplined and responsible approach to your emotions. You may set clear goals and strive for long-term achievements during this lunar transit. Mercury in Virgo makes your thoughts more analytical and detail-oriented, enhancing your communication and problem-solving abilities. Focus on organization and efficiency in your tasks and conversations.

3 Wednesday

With Mercury forming a square aspect to Uranus, you may experience a period of mental restlessness and unpredictability. Your thoughts and ideas may come rapidly and unexpectedly, challenging conventional thinking and pushing you to explore innovative concepts. This aspect can spark flashes of insight and ingenious problem-solving abilities, but it might also lead to scattered thinking and difficulty concentrating.

4 Thursday

As the Moon enters Aquarius, you may notice a shift in your emotional landscape, bringing a sense of curiosity and detachment to your feelings. Aquarius' influence encourages you to approach emotions more intellectually and open-mindedly. During this lunar transition, you might be drawn to socializing and connecting with like-minded individuals who share your interests and values. This transit is an excellent time to embrace your uniqueness and celebrate the diversity in others.

SEPTEMBER

5 Friday

Mars square Jupiter's astrological influence can amplify your confidence and motivation, making you feel invincible and eager to tackle challenges head-on. However, it's essential to be mindful of potential excesses and overconfidence during this transit. The combination of Mars and Jupiter's energies may lead you to take on more than you can handle or act impulsively without considering all the consequences.

6 Saturday

As Uranus turns retrograde, you may experience a period of introspection and reflection on the changes and innovations you've encountered. This planetary shift invites you to revisit past experiences and internalize the lessons they brought, allowing you to understand your growth and evolution better. With the Moon entering Pisces, your emotional sensitivity heightens, and you may find yourself more attuned to the feelings and needs of others.

7 Sunday

Full Moon. You may feel more aware of your inner desires and emotional needs during this phase. This cosmic aspect is an excellent time to release what no longer serves you and embrace new opportunities for growth and transformation. Whether it's a time for celebration or a chance to face challenges, the Full Moon offers a decisive moment to align with your inner wisdom and emotions and to find balance in the cosmic dance between the Moon and the Sun's energies.

SEPTEMBER

8 Monday

As the Moon enters Aries, you may feel a surge of assertive and energetic vibes within you. This lunar transit sparks a sense of initiative and a desire to take charge of your life. You might notice a heightened passion for pursuing your goals and a readiness to face challenges head-on. The Aries Moon encourages you to be bold, confident, and adventurous in your actions. It is an excellent time to start new projects or assert yourself in areas you've been holding back.

---

9 Tuesday

Nurturing your talents and abilities paves the way for exploration and personal development—fresh horizons beckon, carrying you on the winds of change. Rekindling your connection to the wonder and potential of life signals a turning point filled with blessings. Anticipate a boost in the form of exciting news that points you toward social engagement and networking opportunities. Laying the groundwork for social enhancement unlocks encounters with kindred souls.

---

10 Wednesday

As the Moon enters Taurus, you may experience a sense of grounding and stability in your emotions. Taurus' influence brings a calming and nurturing energy, encouraging you to find comfort in life's simple pleasures. During this lunar transit, you may find yourself drawn to the beauty of nature and seeking moments of relaxation and indulgence. Taurus' steadfastness can help you stay focused on your goals, offering a patient and determined approach to achieving them.

---

11 Thursday

As you navigate the path ahead, a sign will guide you toward a stream of possibilities that propel your life in a meaningful direction. In this season of transformation, you are poised to rewrite your life's script. Shedding the old, you become a brighter version of yourself, ready to embrace change and growth. Your journey unfolds with the promise of exciting adventures that beckon you toward realizing your deepest aspirations.

12 Friday

With the Sun forming a sextile to Jupiter, you may experience a boost in confidence and optimism, making it an excellent time to pursue your goals and dreams. This harmonious aspect encourages you to embrace opportunities for growth and expansion, personally and intellectually. As the Moon moves into Gemini, your emotions may become more adaptable and curious, leading to a heightened interest in learning and communication.

13 Saturday

Sun conjunct Mercury alignment enhances your ability to communicate and articulate your thoughts effectively. Your mind is sharp, and you will likely grasp information quickly, making it an excellent time for problem-solving and decision-making. You may share ideas and opinions, leading to engaging conversations and positive interactions. Enjoy the harmonious fusion of the Sun and Mercury's energies to make the most of this mental sharpness and heightened self-awareness.

14 Sunday

As you strengthen your bonds with friends and loved ones, your weekend life becomes a canvas for heartfelt conversations and shared joys. Embrace the cosmic support, and watch as your social circle thrives. Imagine the cosmos as your weekend life coach, guiding you towards meaningful social interactions and deepening bonds. Embrace the cosmic camaraderie, and watch as your weekend becomes a testament to the power of friendship.

SEPTEMBER

15 Monday

As the Moon enters Cancer, you may notice a shift in your emotions, becoming more attuned to your inner feelings and the needs of those around you. Cancer's influence fosters a nurturing and empathetic atmosphere, encouraging you to seek comfort and security in your home and close relationships. During this lunar transit, you may crave spending time with family or loved ones as emotional connections take precedence.

---

16 Tuesday

With Venus forming a harmonious sextile to Mars, you may experience a period of enhanced harmony and attraction in your relationships. This astrological aspect perfectly balances the energies of love and desire, allowing you to express your affections with confidence and sensitivity. Your interactions infuse with a magnetic charm and a willingness to cooperate and find common ground. Embrace the blended energies of Venus and Mars to cultivate loving connections.

---

17 Wednesday

As the Moon moves into Leo, you may notice a shift toward a more confident and expressive emotional state. This lunar transit brings a sense of playfulness and a desire for attention and recognition. Your emotions might be more vibrant and theatrical during this time, prompting you to seek outlets for self-expression and creativity. However, with Mercury opposing Saturn, you might also encounter some mental challenges and communication blockages.

---

18 Thursday

As Mercury moves into Libra, you may seek greater harmony and balance in your thoughts and communication. This astrological shift enhances your ability to see multiple perspectives and find common ground in discussions with others. However, with Mercury opposed to Neptune, you might experience moments of confusion or difficulty in expressing yourself clearly. This aspect can bring a sense of dreaminess and a tendency to be more idealistic.

SEPTEMBER

19 Friday

Mercury forms a trine with Uranus and Pluto so that you may experience mental acuity and transformative thinking. This astrological alignment enhances your ability to grasp innovative ideas and approach problems with a unique perspective. Your communication skills strengthen, and you find it easier to articulate your thoughts and influence others positively. With the Moon's ingress into Virgo, you may feel inclined to focus on practical matters and the details in your daily life.

20 Saturday

When Venus forms a square aspect to Uranus, you may experience a period of unpredictability and emotional turbulence in your relationships and values. This astrological alignment can bring sudden changes and disruptions in your romantic or financial life. You may find yourself craving more freedom and independence in your connections, which could lead to a desire for more unconventional or experimental experiences.

21 Sunday

With the Sun opposed to Saturn, you may feel a sense of restriction and responsibility weighing on you. This astrological aspect can bring challenges and obstacles, making it essential to exercise patience and perseverance. However, with the New Moon and the Moon's ingress into Libra, you have an opportunity for a fresh start and a renewed focus on balance and harmony. This lunar transit fosters a desire for cooperation and diplomacy in your relationships.

SEPTEMBER

22 Monday

As Mars moves into Scorpio, you may feel a surge of intensity and passion in your actions and desires. This astrological event can ignite a deep sense of determination and resourcefulness, urging you to pursue your goals with unwavering focus. The September Equinox marks a seasonal shift, symbolizing a time of balance and reflection. It's an opportune moment to reassess your priorities and realign your energies.

---

23 Tuesday

When the Sun opposes Neptune, you may grapple with confusion and uncertainty. This astrological aspect can bring a sense of disillusionment or a lack of clarity in various areas of your life. It's essential to be cautious of any tendencies towards self-deception or getting lost in unrealistic fantasies. This opposition can make it challenging to see things as they are, leading to potential misunderstandings or a loss of direction.

---

24 Wednesday

With the Sun forming trines to Uranus and Pluto, you may experience transformative energy and self-empowerment. This astrological alignment can inspire you to embrace your uniqueness. The Sun trine Uranus fuels your desire for change and innovation, encouraging you to break free from old patterns and embrace new opportunities. Simultaneously, the Sun trine Pluto empowers you to tap into your inner strength and undergo profound personal growth.

---

25 Thursday

Signs and signals converge to illuminate your path toward exciting prospects. Fresh information infuses your life with heightened potential, enabling swift progress in goal-setting endeavors. Creativity surges, creating a nurturing environment for your talents and gifts to flourish. As you refine your abilities, new avenues open, promising happiness and growth through connections with others who expand your social circle.

SEPTEMBER

26 Friday

As the Moon moves into Sagittarius, you may feel a surge of adventurous and optimistic energy. This lunar transit inspires a desire for exploration and a broader perspective on life. You might be drawn to learning and seeking new experiences that expand your horizons. The Sagittarius Moon encourages you to embrace freedom and spontaneity, making it an ideal time to embark on adventures or engage in activities stimulating your mind and spirit.

27 Saturday

Incoming information commands your attention, guiding you to leave behind the drama and embrace a fresh chapter in your social life. Immersing yourself in expanding your life yields gratifying results. Inspiration and creativity breathe new life into your world, offering fresh options that nurture happiness. You chart a course toward a more balanced and contented environment, replenishing emotional reservoirs through thoughtful dialogues with friends.

28 Sunday

Your thoughtful approach ushers happiness and abundance into your personal life, aligning you with deepening romance and shared journeys. You gracefully orient your life toward heightened romance, passion, and connection. Your adaptability and flexibility nurture stable foundations and pave the way for a rewarding path in your private life. Magic courses through your life, facilitating new goals as you envision possibilities and pursue your dreams.

<u>October</u>

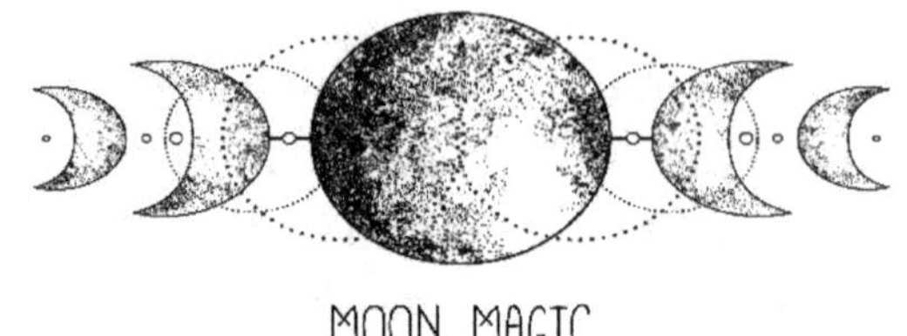

Sun	Mon	Tue	Wed	Thu	Fri	Sat
			1	2	3	4
5	6	7	8	9	10	11
12	13	14	15	16	17	18
19	20	21	22	23	24	25
26	27	28	29	30	31	

NEW MOON

Hunters Moon

SEPTEMBER/OCTOBER

29 Monday

As the Moon enters Capricorn, you may notice a shift towards a more practical and disciplined emotional state. This lunar transit fosters a sense of responsibility and a focus on long-term goals. Your emotions become more grounded and organized, urging you to take a structured approach to your feelings and relationships. This transit is a favorable time to set clear intentions and work diligently towards your ambitions.

30 Tuesday

You stand to gain from upcoming opportunities as they align with a refreshing period encouraging growth, advancement, and rising prospects. Learning a new area becomes a winning formula that deepens your knowledge and hones your skills. It marks the beginning of an inspirational phase, illuminating your career path and unveiling new possibilities for growth. This ushers in an active period of working with your abilities.

1 Wednesday

As the Moon enters Aquarius, you may feel a stronger desire for independence and a connection to your broader community. This astrological influence encourages you to think outside the box and embrace your unique perspective. However, Mercury square Jupiter has a potential for over-optimism and grandiose thinking. This aspect can lead to hasty decisions or an inclination to overlook details. It's crucial to balance visionary ideas and practical considerations.

2 Thursday

You unearth new life opportunities that spill over into your situation, ushering in a generous period for nurturing your creativity. This extended period of growth enhances your sense of security as you embark on transformation on multiple levels. A journey of rejuvenation paves the way for an open road of possibilities that entice you forward, helping you establish stable foundations that feel grounded and complete.

October

3 Friday

As you approach the weekend, the cosmic energies align to enhance your social life. The universe acts as your social navigator, steering you toward delightful connections. Your weekend life becomes a symphony of shared laughter, love, and camaraderie, with each note representing the strength of your bonds with others. Trust in the cosmic friendships, and watch as your social world thrives. It's as though the universe set the stage for moments of laughter and camaraderie.

---

4 Saturday

As the Moon moves into Pisces, you may experience heightened emotional sensitivity and a deeper connection to your intuition. This astrological influence encourages you to embrace your imagination and tap into the more subtle aspects of your feelings. Pisces' energy fosters empathy and compassion, making it an ideal time to connect with others on a soulful level. During this lunar transit, you might find solace in creative and artistic pursuits and moments of self-reflection.

---

5 Sunday

Beautiful symmetry manifests in your life, nurturing grounded foundations and ushering in a highly creative and expressive period. You embark on a voyage of your creation, working with your creativity to find happiness and self-improvement, guiding you in nurturing and growing your talents, extending your reach, and listening to your instincts open doors to a positive and transformative chapter in your life.

OCTOBER

6 Monday

You may feel dynamic energy and assertiveness as the Moon moves into Aries. This astrological influence encourages you to take the initiative and approach tasks enthusiastically and confidently. Your emotions become more spontaneous, and you might find yourself drawn to activities that involve physical movement or challenges. With Mercury entering Scorpio, your thinking becomes more investigative and introspective.

7 Tuesday

During a Full Moon, you may experience heightened emotions and a sense of culmination in various aspects of your life. This astrological phase marks a time of heightened awareness and a need to confront truths or issues that have been hidden or ignored. However, Mercury square Pluto has the potential for intense and sometimes challenging communication. This aspect can bring power struggles in conversations and a tendency to be overly critical or suspicious.

8 Wednesday

Moon ingress Taurus astrological shift encourages you to indulge in sensory experiences and find joy in the simple luxuries of life. Taurus' energy fosters a connection to nature and the material world, making it an excellent time to enjoy delicious food, soothing music, or any other sensory delights that bring you contentment. Additionally, with Venus sextile Jupiter, your relationships and social interactions may be harmonious and uplifting.

9 Thursday

Incoming information contributes to building more grounded foundations in your life. You discover an area that refills your emotional reserves, casting a lighter hue over your life. Blossoming activity attracts new options, paving the way for a journey offering room for growth and a unique path forward. Indeed, this journey enables you to express your talents creatively and effectively, leading to personal growth.

October

10 Friday

As the Moon moves into Gemini, you may feel a heightened curiosity and a desire for mental stimulation. This astrological influence encourages you to engage in conversations, explore new ideas, and seek out diverse sources of information. Gemini's energy fosters versatility and adaptability in your emotions, making it a favorable time to connect with others and share your thoughts. You might notice your mind becoming more agile and open to various viewpoints.

11 Saturday

When Venus opposes Saturn, you may encounter challenges and limitations in your relationships and matters of the heart. This astrological aspect can bring a sense of distance or coldness to your interactions. You might experience delays or obstacles in your romantic endeavors, leading to feelings of isolation or disappointment. It's essential to be patient and realistic in your expectations, as this opposition can test the strength of your connections.

12 Sunday

As the Moon moves into Cancer, you may notice a shift towards a more nurturing and emotional state. This astrological influence encourages you to connect with your feelings and seek comfort in familiar settings. Cancer's energy fosters a deep sense of empathy and a desire for close connections with loved ones. During this lunar transit, you might find solace in spending time at home or engaging in activities that evoke a sense of security and emotional well-being.

OCTOBER

13 Monday

With Venus moving into Libra, you may experience a shift towards a greater emphasis on harmony and balance. This astrological transition encourages you to seek out beauty, whether in your surroundings or the company of others. Libra's energy fosters a desire for companionship and a sense of unity, making it an excellent time to focus on creating peaceful and fair interactions at social gatherings and cultivating connections that bring a sense of equilibrium.

14 Tuesday

As Venus opposes Neptune, you may encounter a period of heightened romantic idealism and sensitivity. This astrological aspect can bring a touch of enchantment to your relationships, but be cautious of potential illusions or unrealistic expectations. Simultaneously, a sense of empowerment and transformation may emerge with Pluto turning direct. This shift encourages you to embrace your inner strength and initiate changes that align with your authentic self.

15 Wednesday

Noteworthy changes loom on the horizon, heralding a journey characterized by growth and advancement. The forthcoming events promise to deliver fresh information, granting you an open road to realize your dreams and embark on a journey of progress. Nurturing your talents enables you to venture into unique and rewarding domains while your evolving situation brings opportunities to share your expertise. The knock of opportunity signifies that change is underway.

16 Thursday

As the Moon moves into Virgo, you may feel a shift towards practicality and a desire for order in your emotions. This astrological transition encourages you to focus on the details and seek efficiency in your daily routines. Virgo's energy fosters a sense of organization and a heightened awareness of health and well-being. During this lunar transit, you might find solace in tasks that require precision and attention to detail and in activities that promote self-care.

October

17 Friday

When the Sun forms a square aspect to Jupiter, you might experience a period of enthusiasm and expansion. This astrological aspect can bring a sense of optimism and a desire to pursue new opportunities and experiences. However, there is a potential for overindulgence or taking on too much at once. Balancing your ambitions and practicality is essential, as this square may lead to unrealistic expectations.

18 Saturday

Changes help reboot your life, creating ample opportunities to connect with friends. This journey expands your world as you share experiences and thoughts with others, introducing a broader range of possibilities that foster lively conversations, social engagement, and happiness. It ushers in a time of change and inspiration, elevating the goodness in your social life. Your life is ripening with fresh possibilities that draw rising prospects into your world.

19 Sunday

As the Moon moves into Libra, you may notice a shift towards a greater emphasis on harmony and relationships. This astrological influence encourages you to seek balance and cooperation in your interactions with others. Libra's energy fosters a desire for fairness and a willingness to compromise to create harmonious connections. During this lunar transit, you feel attuned to the feelings of those around you, making it an ideal time for engaging in heartfelt conversations.

OCTOBER

20 Monday

With Mercury and Mars joining, you may experience a surge of mental energy and assertiveness. This astrological alignment enhances your ability to express your thoughts. Your communication becomes more direct and decisive, making it a favorable time to engage in debates or discussions that require quick thinking and assertive responses. This conjunction also boosts your ability to initiate new projects and tackle tasks that require mental agility.

21 Tuesday

During a New Moon, you may experience a sense of fresh beginnings and the opportunity to set new intentions. This astrological phase marks the start of a new lunar cycle, inviting you to plant seeds of growth and transformation. As the Moon moves into Scorpio, your emotions may deepen, and you may find yourself drawn to introspection and uncovering hidden truths. Scorpio's energy encourages you to embrace the power of regeneration and release what no longer serves you.

22 Wednesday

With Neptune moving into Pisces, you may notice a shift towards a more dreamy and intuitive atmosphere. This astrological transition encourages you to tap into your imagination and embrace a greater connection to the spiritual and mystical realms. Pisces' energy fosters empathy and a deeper understanding of the subtle nuances of emotions. During this transit, you might find yourself drawn to creative and artistic pursuits that allow you to express your inner world.

23 Thursday

As the Sun moves into Scorpio, you may experience a shift to transformative energy. This astrological transition encourages you to delve deep into your emotions and uncover hidden truths. Scorpio's energy fosters authenticity and a willingness to confront light and shadow aspects of yourself and your surroundings. During this solar transit, you might be in introspection and self-discovery mode, seeking an understanding of your motivations and desires.

OCTOBER

24 Friday

Moon ingress Sagittarius astrological influence encourages you to embrace new horizons and broaden your perspective. However, the Sun square Pluto aspect can bring intensity and potential power struggles. It's essential to be cautious about controlling situations or manipulating others. Concurrently, with Mercury trine Jupiter, your communication skills may shine, and your thoughts may be more optimistic and expansive.

25 Saturday

Mercury trine Saturn astrological alignment empowers you with a focused and systematic approach to your thoughts and communication. Your mind becomes more organized and capable of tackling complex tasks with precision. This trine encourages you to focus on details and carefully plan your actions. It's a favorable time for making long-term decisions and engaging in structured conversations. This trine fosters a willingness to pay attention to details, contributing to success.

26 Sunday

As the Moon moves into Capricorn, you may notice a shift towards a more disciplined and goal-oriented emotional state. This astrological influence encourages you to prioritize your responsibilities and take a structured approach to your feelings. Capricorn's energy fosters a desire for achievement and a willingness to work hard to attain your ambitions. During this lunar transit, you might find satisfaction in tackling tasks that require diligence and dedication.

OCTOBER

27 Monday

Animated discussions in a group setting elevate your happiness and well-being. The upcoming events promise enriching experiences and abundant growth. A journey unfolds, weaving contentment and joy into your life's tapestry. It signifies a shift toward an open road of endless possibilities. Your readiness to craft and pursue your vision ignites a realm brimming with captivating options. Focusing on developing and designing goals unlocks a gateway to advancement.

28 Tuesday

With Mars forming a trine to Jupiter, you may experience increased energy, enthusiasm, and confidence. This astrological alignment empowers you to take bold actions and pursue your goals with vigor. Your assertiveness holds optimism and expansiveness, encouraging you to take calculated risks and embrace growth opportunities. This trine can amplify your motivation and drive, making it an excellent time to tackle challenges and venture into new territories.

29 Wednesday

As the Moon moves into Aquarius, you may notice a shift towards a more intellectual and innovative emotional state. This astrological influence encourages embracing a broader perspective and engaging with progressive ideas. With Mercury forming a trine to Neptune, your thoughts and communication become more intuitive and creative, allowing for open-minded discussions and the potential for spiritual insights.

30 Thursday

With Mercury forming a sextile to Pluto, you may experience heightened mental intensity and a deeper understanding of complex matters. This astrological alignment empowers you to uncover hidden truths beneath the surface. Your thinking becomes more profound and wise, allowing you to engage in transformative conversations and research. This sextile encourages you to explore topics that intrigue you and engage in meaningful discussions.

<u>NOVEMBER</u>

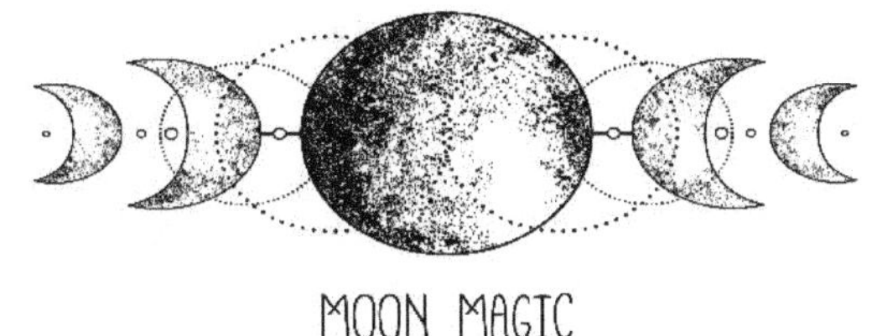

Sun	Mon	Tue	Wed	Thu	Fri	Sat
						1
2	3	4	5	6	7	8
9	10	11	12	13	14	15
16	17	18	19	20	21	22
23	24	25	26	27	28	29
30						

NEW MOON

<u>Beaver Moon</u>

OCTOBER/NOVEMBER

31 Friday

As the Moon moves into Pisces, your emotions become more sensitive and dreamy. This astrological influence encourages you to connect with your inner world and embrace your intuitive side. Pisces' energy fosters empathy and compassion, making it a favorable time to communicate with your emotions and those of others. You might notice a heightened imagination and a desire to engage in creative and spiritual activities.

1 Saturday

The universe encourages you to express your artistic talents through the written word, the stroke of a paintbrush, the melody of music, or any other creative endeavor that stirs your soul. Inspiration flows like stardust, infusing your creations with magic. Celestial energies inspire a harmonious and nurturing environment akin to a heavenly abode. Whether through redecorating your living space or strengthening the bonds with your loved ones, the cosmos smiles.

2 Sunday

With the Moon moving into Aries, this astrological shift encourages you to take initiative and enthusiastically pursue your passions. However, with Venus square Jupiter, there's potential for extravagance and overindulgence in matters of love and pleasure. This aspect can bring a sense of optimism and a need to exercise caution when making impulsive decisions. Despite potential challenges, the Aries Moon's energy empowers you to face obstacles head-on and initiate change.

NOVEMBER

3 Monday

News arrives, carrying a sense of providence into your life and opening the door to new possibilities. It propels you toward a meaningful area that sparks movement and discovery, helping you map a strategy for future contingencies. A curious path beckons, offering to elevate your skills and lay the foundation for a grounded and progressive chapter. It aligns with a broader theme of change that emphasizes knowledge development and significantly enhances your life.

4 Tuesday

With Mars forming a trine to Neptune, you may experience a period of heightened creativity and inspired action. This astrological alignment empowers you to channel your energy into imaginative and spiritually driven pursuits. As Mars moves into Sagittarius, your drive becomes infused with a sense of adventure and a desire to explore new horizons. Meanwhile, the Moon's ingress into Taurus brings a grounding influence, encouraging you to seek comfort and stability.

5 Wednesday

During a Full Moon, you may experience a heightened sense of culmination and intensity in your emotions. This astrological phase illuminates hidden aspects, clarifying your feelings and situations. The Full Moon marks a moment of potential revelation and awareness, where feelings come to the forefront, and you might gain insights into areas of your life previously obscured. It's a time to reflect on your intentions set during the New Moon and evaluate your progress.

6 Thursday

With Mars forming a sextile to Pluto, you may experience increased determination and empowerment. This astrological alignment lets you tap into your inner strength and take strategic actions toward goals. As the Moon moves into Gemini, your emotions may become more curious and adaptable. This lunar transition encourages diverse interests and conversations. Simultaneously, Venus moving into Scorpio adds a touch of intensity to your relationships and desires.

NOVEMBER

7 Friday

The universe's plan for you involves fresh opportunities on the horizon, each akin to celestial gifts sent to guide you toward personal growth and positive change. The cosmic patterns currently in play focus on your social connections. In this heavenly orchestra, your relationships with kindred spirits are destined to deepen, offering a profound sense of belonging and fulfillment. Prepare for heartwarming conversations and shared laughter beneath the vast canvas of the starry night.

8 Saturday

The Uranus-Taurus influence prompts you to embrace change in your values, while the Venus-Pluto square challenges you to navigate relationships with authenticity. The Cancer Moon encourages you to seek emotional comfort and connection. Embrace the Uranus ingress into Taurus to embrace innovation, use the Venus-Pluto square to transform relationships healthily, and allow the Cancer Moon to guide nurturing emotional well-being in this dynamic period.

9 Sunday

When Mercury turns retrograde, you may experience potential communication challenges. This astrological phenomenon often prompts you to review and reflect on your thoughts, plans, and interactions. During this time, misunderstandings and technical glitches can be more common, so exercising caution and double-checking details. While it might feel like a slow-down, this retrograde period offers an opportunity to revisit unresolved matters and gain a new perspective.

10 Monday

As the Moon moves into Leo, you may notice a shift towards a more expressive and confident emotional state. This astrological transition encourages you to embrace your inner creativity and seek out activities that bring you joy and recognition. Leo's energy fosters a desire for attention and a willingness to shine in the spotlight. During this lunar transit, you might find yourself drawn to social interactions and opportunities that allow you to showcase your talents.

11 Tuesday

As Jupiter turns retrograde, you may experience a period of internal reflection and reassessment of your expansion and growth. This astrological event encourages you to review your goals and aspirations, considering whether they align with your values and beliefs. While this retrograde phase might feel like a slowdown, it offers an opportunity to delve deeper into your personal and spiritual development. It's a time to revisit your plans and seek wisdom from within.

12 Wednesday

With Mercury conjunct Mars, you may experience heightened mental activity and assertiveness. This astrological alignment empowers you to express your thoughts and ideas confidently and directly. Your mind becomes sharper and quicker, making it a favorable time for problem-solving and initiating discussions. As the Moon moves into Virgo, your emotions may become more practical and focused on details.

13 Thursday

You enter a radiant phase where creativity is your compass and work diligently to achieve positive results. These attractive options leave you optimistic, ushering in a vibrant environment fostering growth and progress. Your focus sharpens on improving your circumstances, and you boldly push past barriers, setting your sights on achieving your goals. This winning chapter nurtures life and fosters talent development as you pour energy into creating a significant and joyous area.

14 Friday

Engaging in the design of your life fosters greater optimism. As you embark on the journey to develop your goals, you find renewed hope in crafting a vision that yields tangible results. A positive change is poised to bloom, ushering in bursts of inspiration that facilitate your growth and prosperity. The path you embark upon captures the essence of creativity. News arrives, demanding your consideration and offering a gateway to fresh energy.

15 Saturday

As the Moon moves into Libra, you may notice a shift towards a greater focus on harmony and balance in your emotions and interactions. This astrological transition encourages you to seek cooperation in your relationships. Libra's energy fosters a desire for companionship and a willingness to find common ground. During this lunar transition, you might find yourself drawn to social activities and engaging in conversations that create understanding and unity.

16 Sunday

Optimizing your life and setting goals for your home life brings a rejuvenated perspective. This shift helps you shed turbulent energy and cultivate fresh possibilities. Engaging with your creativity propels you through a period of honing and enhancing your life. This newfound inspiration illuminates projects that promise growth and opportunity. You unveil an area of interest where much can be uncovered by staying informed and exploring broader possibilities.

NOVEMBER

17 Monday

With the Sun forming trines to Jupiter and Saturn, you may experience a balanced growth and stability period. This astrological alignment allows you to expand your horizons while maintaining a practical and disciplined approach to your goals. As Mercury sextiles Pluto, your communication becomes more insightful, allowing you to engage in meaningful conversations and delve into deep subjects. With the Moon moving into Scorpio, your emotions are turning introspective.

18 Tuesday

Significant changes on the horizon connect you with a prosperous period of growth. Being open to discovering new opportunities brings effective options into focus. An alternate avenue opens up, inviting you to explore a unique path that fosters your abilities and deepens your talents. Immersing yourself in creatively inspiring areas keeps life vibrant and fresh. This lively chapter opens the door to new adventures.

19 Wednesday

As Mercury moves into Scorpio, you may experience more probing thinking. This astrological transition encourages you to uncover hidden truths beneath the surface. The Mercury-Uranus opposition can bring unexpected twists to your thoughts and communication, fostering a need for flexibility and adaptability. However, with Mercury trine Neptune, your intuition and creativity are heightened, allowing you to express yourself in imaginative and empathetic ways.

20 Thursday

During a New Moon, you may experience fresh beginnings and opportunities. This astrological phase marks a time of setting intentions and initiating new projects. With the Sun conjunct with Mercury, there's an emphasis on communication and clarity. As Mercury moves into Sagittarius, your thinking becomes expansive. The Uranus sextile Neptune aspect combines innovation and intuition, offering insights to bridge between the practical and the ethereal.

NOVEMBER

21 Friday

With the Sun opposed to Uranus, you may experience unexpected changes and a desire for liberation from routine. This astrological aspect can bring about a sense of restlessness and a need for personal freedom. Embrace this energy to embrace new perspectives and break free from the limitations that have held you back. On the other hand, the Sun trine Neptune aspect adds a touch of inspiration and creativity to your experiences.

22 Saturday

As the Sun moves into Sagittarius, you may sense a shift towards more adventurous and expansive energy. This astrological transition encourages you to embrace new perspectives and seek growth opportunities. With Mercury forming a trine to Saturn, your thoughts and communication become more disciplined and focused. As the Moon moves into Capricorn, your emotions may align with a practical and determined approach.

23 Sunday

With the Sun forming a sextile to Pluto, you may experience a period of empowerment and transformation. This astrological alignment empowers you to tap into your inner strength and make positive changes. The Sun's sextile to Pluto encourages you to embrace your power and delve into deeper layers of your psyche. It is a time when you have the potential to uncover hidden truths and shed light on concealed matters.

NOVEMBER

24 Monday

This significant period of change may initially feel unsettling. However, the events on the horizon promise newfound possibilities, growth, and progress. They mark the inception of a vibrant and productive phase that nurtures happiness and ushers in the magic of transformation. Life brims with potential, ready to bloom as a bustling chapter unfolds, turning the corner toward a more prosperous future. A positive trend ushers a fresh start, infusing you with confidence.

25 Tuesday

With Mercury forming a conjunction with Venus, you may experience a period of enhanced social interactions and expressive communication. This astrological alignment empowers you to express your thoughts and feelings with charm and grace. Your conversations may have a harmonious and affectionate tone, making it a favorable time for connecting. As the Moon moves into Aquarius, your emotions may focus more on intellectual pursuits.

26 Wednesday

With Venus forming trines to Jupiter and Saturn, you may experience a period of harmonious and balanced energies in your relationships and values. This astrological alignment gives you a sense of abundance and stability in love, beauty, and resources. The Venus trine Jupiter cosmic interplay encourages you to embrace optimism and open-heartedness, fostering positive interactions and a greater appreciation for life's pleasures.

27 Thursday

On Thanksgiving Day, as the Moon moves into Pisces, you might find yourself embracing a sense of compassion and gratitude. This astrological transition encourages you to connect with your emotions and appreciate the beauty in the world around you. Pisces' energy fosters a desire for unity and spiritual reflection. It is an ideal time to express gratitude for your life's blessings and share moments of love and empathy with others.

November

28 Friday

As Saturn turns direct, you may sense a shift in the cosmic energies influencing your life. This astrological event often brings a feeling of increased structure and discipline. Saturn, known as the taskmaster of the zodiac, can now provide clearer pathways for you to pursue your long-term goals and ambitions. Delays or obstacles you've encountered might begin to lift, allowing you to move forward with incredible determination and a sense of purpose.

29 Saturday

As Mercury turns direct, you may experience a sense of relief and clarity in your communication and thought processes. This astrological event marks the end of a potentially challenging retrograde period, during which misunderstandings, delays, and miscommunications may have been more common. With Mercury resuming its forward motion, you can expect smoother interactions, clearer thinking, and a reduced likelihood of technical glitches or delays in everyday tasks.

30 Sunday

With the Moon moving into Aries, you might feel a surge of energy and assertiveness. With Venus entering Sagittarius, your approach to love and pleasure becomes more adventurous and open-minded. Embrace the Aries Moon's power to take initiative while using the Venus-Uranus opposition as an opportunity for personal growth and transformation. Let the Venus-Neptune trine inspire you to connect with others on a deeper, more spiritual level.

DECEMBER

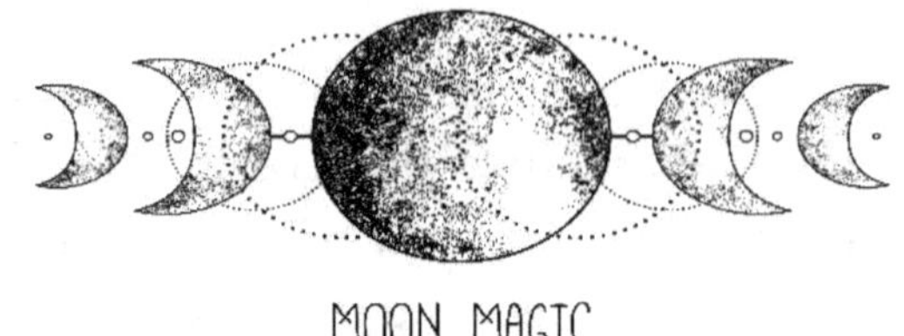

Sun	Mon	Tue	Wed	Thu	Fri	Sat
	1	2	3	4	5	6
7	8	9	10	11	12	13
14	15	16	17	18	19	20
21	22	23	24	25	26	27
28	29	30	31			

NEW MOON

COLD MOON

DECEMBER

1 Monday

December brings a social season with companionship and romantic possibilities. It lifts the veil on an inspiring environment ripe with blessings. Serendipity takes the lead, fostering connections. Meaningful conversations weave threads of happiness and harmony, opening the door to a unique and fulfilling journey tailored to your life. It breathes new life into your social bonds, drawing renewal and infusing happiness into moments shared with your friends.

2 Tuesday

With the Moon moving into Taurus, you might experience a shift towards a more grounded and sensual emotional state. This astrological transition encourages you to seek comfort and stability in your surroundings and relationships. The Venus sextile Pluto aspect adds depth and intensity to your interactions and desires. It's when you may feel a stronger connection to your passions and a desire for more profound relationships.

3 Wednesday

Your discerning and accountable nature harnesses the energy of karma to your advantage. Trusting your intuition empowers you to make fair and just decisions. You embark on a journey aligned with your core values, opening up pathways for career growth, with a new role beckoning to advance your life. As you surge forward, developing critical aspects of your life reveals opportunities for growth that nurture rising prospects.

4 Thursday

With the Moon moving into Gemini and the arrival of a Full Moon, you may experience a heightened curiosity and mental activity. This astrological phase marks a time of culmination and realization, urging you to balance your emotions and intellect. Gemini's energy fosters communication and a willingness to explore new ideas and perspectives. The Full Moon's radiance sheds light on aspects that require attention, inviting you to embrace the future with clarity.

DECEMBER

5 Friday

A surprise invitation emerges, drawing you into budding friendships and revitalizing your social life. Friends extend their hands in camaraderie, engaging you in spirited conversations and news sharing. This lively atmosphere ushers in a phase of life where people rally around you, offering unwavering support and companionship. Encouraged by these rising prospects, you find yourself uplifted, basking in an aura of lightness and happiness that propels you forward.

6 Saturday

Embrace the Cancer Moon's energy to create a warm and supportive atmosphere for yourself and your loved ones. Allow Mercury's trine to Neptune to inspire compassionate conversations and foster a deeper emotional connection with those around you. Use this cosmic synergy to nurture your needs and engage in heartfelt exchanges as you navigate this period of emotional depth and intuitive communication.

7 Sunday

An upsurge of potential within your social sphere is a wellspring of inspiration and encouragement. This backdrop sets the stage for forging new friendships and expanding your circle of acquaintances. Spending time with kindred spirits infuses your life with vitality, laying the groundwork for robust foundations that facilitate growth and happiness. Engaging in thoughtful discussions ignites a spark of possibility.

DECEMBER

8 Monday

A fast-paced environment draws advancement into your life. Refining your skills and cultivating knowledge unlock the code to a bright chapter. Your disciplined actions, drive, and perseverance propel you toward outstanding achievements as you plan your path and set intentions. Your dedication to life improvement yields dividends as you pivot away from obstacles and channel your energy into achieving essential objectives.

9 Tuesday

With Mars forming a square to Saturn, you might encounter frustration and obstacles. This astrological aspect can clash between your desires and your limitations or responsibilities. It could feel like you're trying to move forward, but external or internal forces are holding you back. This square aspect can be a challenging period, but it also provides an opportunity for patience, discipline, and strategic planning.

10 Wednesday

With the Moon moving into Virgo, you may notice a shift towards a more analytical and detail-oriented emotional state. This astrological transition encourages you to focus on practical matters and pay attention to the finer points of your daily life. Virgo's energy fosters a desire for organization and efficiency. Additionally, Neptune's forward movement enhances your creativity and ability to tap into your inner wisdom.

11 Thursday

With Mercury forming a trine to Neptune, you may experience a period of heightened intuition and imaginative thinking. This astrological alignment empowers you to tap into your inner wisdom and express yourself with empathy and creativity. Your communication becomes more attuned to the subtleties of emotions and the power of inspiration. As Mercury moves into Sagittarius, your thinking becomes more expansive and open-minded.

DECEMBER

12 Friday

With the Moon moving into Libra, you may notice a shift towards a more harmonious and balanced emotional state. This astrological transition encourages you to seek fairness and cooperation in your interactions with others. Libra's energy fosters a desire for companionship and a willingness to find common ground. During this lunar transit, you might find yourself drawn to social activities and engaging in conversations that create understanding and unity.

13 Saturday

With Mercury forming a sextile to Pluto, you might find your communication and thinking taking on a more profound and insightful quality. This astrological aspect encourages you to delve deep into matters, seeking hidden truths and uncovering insights. It's as if your mental faculties are given a surge of transformative power. You'll find engaging in conversations that touch upon profound subjects easier, and your ability to persuade and influence others may be heightened.

14 Sunday

With Mars forming a square to Neptune, you might find yourself confused and uncertain in your actions and ambitions. This astrological aspect can bring about a sense of frustration and a lack of clarity in pursuing your goals. It's as if the path ahead is shrouded in mist, making it challenging to make decisive moves. This cosmic influence can sap your energy and motivation, leaving you somewhat adrift.

15 Monday

As the Moon moves into Scorpio, you may sense a deepening of emotions and a desire for introspection. This astrological shift encourages you to delve into your innermost feelings and explore the layers of your psyche. Scorpio's energy fosters intensity, passion, and a need to uncover hidden truths. Additionally, with Mars entering Capricorn, your drive and ambition become more focused and disciplined.

16 Tuesday

A significant shift offers a new and exciting chapter. It helps you shed any lingering heavy vibes and propels you toward a period of nurturing your talents and developing your abilities. This creatively rich process inspires growth and allows you to discard elements that are no longer relevant, embarking on a journey filled with expansion and happiness. As positive results continue to gravitate toward you, the essence of manifestation envelops your life.

17 Wednesday

With the Sun forming a square to Saturn, this astrological aspect can challenge your sense of self-expression and vitality. It may feel like your goals and ambitions are met with resistance or that external circumstances are holding you back. However, as the Moon moves into Sagittarius, you'll sense a desire for exploration and a need for freedom. This lunar transit encourages you to look beyond limitations and seek new experiences that broaden your horizons.

18 Thursday

A journey of expansion facilitates meeting new companions, opening the door to exploring a wide vista of refreshing potential within your social circles. Fundamental changes propel a shift forward, offering fresh opportunities for your life. This transformation paves the way for developing friendships and enhancing security in your social life. A refreshing period of lively conversations creates a gateway to a happier environment.

DECEMBER

19 Friday

Behind the scenes, alchemy is at play, offering you an opportunity to actively engage in developing your goals. A change of pace brings expansion and paves the way for an intriguing phase in your life. As your circumstances improve, it offers a chance to nurture your social life. Friendships flourish, ushering in new opportunities. The companionship promotes your well-being and happiness, creating a fertile ground for rising prospects.

20 Saturday

With the arrival of a New Moon, you stand at the threshold of fresh beginnings and a chance to set new intentions for the future. This astrological phase marks a clean slate, urging you to plant the seeds of your aspirations and watch them grow in the coming lunar cycle. As the Moon moves into Capricorn, you'll likely feel a call to approach these new beginnings with a sense of discipline and determination, focusing on your long-term goals and responsibilities.

21 Sunday

With the Sun forming a square to Neptune, you might find that a fog of confusion envelops your sense of direction during this astrological aspect. It's as if reality blurs at the edges, making it challenging to assert your will with clarity. Your dreams and ideals clash with the demands of everyday life, leading to uncertainty. Similarly, Venus's square to Saturn may restrict your relationships and pleasures as you grapple with the need for structure and responsibility.

December

22 Monday

With the Moon moving into Aquarius, you might notice a shift towards a more independent and forward-thinking emotional state. This astrological transition encourages you to embrace your uniqueness and explore unconventional ideas. Aquarius' energy fosters a sense of freedom and a desire to connect with like-minded individuals who share your interests and values. You may be drawn to humanitarian causes and a greater sense of community.

23 Tuesday

Lovely changes promote a growth-oriented phase in your life, allowing you to shine a pioneering trail toward your dreams. It sets the stage for expanding your world outwardly, with a surge of inspiring options on the horizon. This period invites mingling with friends, blending ideas with thoughtful discussions. A more prosperous life experience unfolds as communication boosts your life, harmonizing with friends and companions who support your journey.

24 Wednesday

With Venus forming a square to Neptune, you might find yourself navigating some complexities in matters of the heart and personal values. This astrological aspect can create a sense of ambiguity and illusion in your relationships and desires. It's crucial to exercise caution and avoid making significant decisions based solely on idealized perceptions during this period. Simultaneously, as Venus moves into Capricorn, you'll experience a more grounded approach to love.

25 Thursday

As the Moon glides into Pisces on Christmas Day, you may experience a heightened sense of empathy, spirituality, and emotional connection. This astrological transition creates an atmosphere of tenderness and a desire for peace and harmony in your celebrations. Pisces' energy fosters a deep appreciation for the soul's beauty and the season's magic. It's a perfect time to engage in acts of kindness, express your love for family and friends, and find joy in the art of giving.

DECEMBER

26 Friday

Home and family, like prominent constellations in your celestial journey, bask in the radiance of the cosmic spotlight. The divine energies inspire you to create a harmonious and nurturing environment within the sanctuary of your home. Whether it involves redecorating your space or strengthening familial bonds, the cosmos blesses your domestic aspirations. This enriching chapter lays the groundwork, bringing lighter energy to chart a course toward happiness.

---

27 Saturday

As the Moon enters fiery Aries, you may feel energy and motivation coursing. This astrological shift encourages a more assertive and adventurous attitude. Aries' energy is bold, impulsive, and forward-looking, inspiring you to take initiative and enthusiastically pursue your goals. You might be eager to start new projects, embrace challenges, and assert your individuality. It's a great time to channel this spirited energy into activities that require courage and leadership.

---

28 Sunday

You enrich your life's narrative by embracing new possibilities and welcoming change. Exciting news unfolds, unveiling an upgraded chapter brimming with sunshine and happiness. A captivating journey with a well-suited social aspect comes into view, widening your social circle and nurturing the growth of enriching bonds. This aspect breathes new life into your social sphere, instigating a transformation and laying the foundation for a meaningful journey.

---

29 Monday

As the Moon gracefully moves into Taurus, you may notice a shift towards a more grounded and stable emotional state. This astrological transition encourages you to seek comfort and security in your surroundings and to connect with your senses on a deeper level. Taurus' energy fosters a desire for peace and tranquility, making it an ideal time to indulge in life's simple pleasures, whether enjoying a delicious meal, spending time in nature or surrounding yourself with beauty.

30 Tuesday

When Mercury squares Saturn, communication and decision-making can often feel like an uphill battle. You may find that your thoughts and ideas are met with resistance or obstacles, making it challenging to express yourself effectively. This aspect can bring a sense of self-doubt and a tendency to be overly critical of your abilities. Your mind may dwell on limitations and responsibilities, causing mental stress and anxiety.

31 Wednesday

On New Year's Eve, you may experience a noticeable shift in your emotional energy when the Moon ingresses into Gemini. Gemini is an air sign known for its curiosity and versatility, and this lunar placement can make you feel more mentally agile and friendly. You'll likely be in the mood for engaging in conversations and connecting with friends. It is when your emotions may be expressed through words, and you might find it easier to articulate them.

1 Thursday

On New Year's Day, Mercury's ingress into Capricorn and its square aspect to Neptune may bring a sense of practicality and ambition to your thoughts and communication style. You'll likely be more focused on setting goals, making plans, and mapping out your aspirations for the year ahead. However, the challenging square with Neptune could introduce a layer of confusion or idealism to your thinking, making it crucial to approach resolutions with a dose of realism.

Astrology, Tarot & Horoscope Books.

Mystic Cat

Ohoroscope@Hotmail.com

www.ingramcontent.com/pod-product-compliance
Lightning Source LLC
LaVergne TN
LVHW080310110826
845155LV00023B/108
* 9 7 8 1 9 2 2 8 1 3 3 9 8 *